MARMARIS TRAVEL GUIDE 2025

Discover the Pearl of the Turkish Riviera: A Comprehensive Guide

Michael Bradley

Copyright © 2024 Michael Bradley

All rights reserved.

No part of this book may be reproduced, stored in a retrieval system, or transmitted in any form or by any means, electronic, mechanical, photocopying, recording, or otherwise, without the prior written permission of the copyright owner.

TABLE OF CONTENTS

Chapter 1: Introduction to Marmaris   6
   1.1 Welcome to Marmaris   6
   1.2 Brief History of Marmaris   7
   1.3 Overview of Marmaris Today   9

Chapter 2: Getting to Marmaris   11
   2.1 By Air: Nearest Airports and Transfers   11
   2.2 By Road: Bus and Car Travel Options   13
   2.3 By Sea: Ferry and Cruise Routes   14
      Key Takeaways   16

Chapter 3: Where to Stay in Marmaris   17
   3.1 Luxury Resorts and Hotels   17
   3.2 Budget-Friendly Accommodation   19
   3.3 Family-Friendly Stays   20
   3.4 Alternative Lodgings: Villas and Apartments   21

Chapter 4: Exploring Marmaris Town   24
   4.1 Marmaris Marina and Promenade   24
   4.2 Marmaris Castle and Museum   26
   4.3 Grand Bazaar: Local Shopping Experience   28

Chapter 5: Beaches and Waterfront Activities   31
   5.1 Best Beaches in Marmaris   31
   5.2 Water Sports: Jet Skiing, Parasailing, and More 33
   5.3 Relaxing Beach Clubs   36

Chapter 6: Day Trips and Excursions   39
   6.1 Cleopatra Island (Sedir Island)   39
   6.2 Dalyan River Cruise and Mud Baths   41
   6.3 Village Tours: Traditional Turkish Life   43

CHAPTER 7: Outdoor Adventures   **46**

  7.1 Hiking Trails and Nature Walks   46
      Popular Hiking Trails   46
      Key Highlights   47
      Tips for Hiking in Marmaris   48
  7.2 Off-Road Safari Experiences   48
      What to Expect   48
      Top Safari Experiences   49
      Why Go Off-Roading?   49
      Preparation Tips   50
  7.3 Cycling Around Marmaris   50
      Best Cycling Routes   51
      Cycling Highlights   51
      Cycling Events   51
      Tips for Cyclists   52

CHAPTER 8: Cultural and Historical Landmarks   **53**

  8.1 Ancient Ruins Near Marmaris   53
  8.2 Local Mosques and Religious Sites   55
  8.3 Traditional Turkish Baths   58

CHAPTER 9: Dining in Marmaris   **61**

  9.1 Authentic Turkish Cuisine   61
  9.2 Seafood Restaurants by the Coast   64
  9.3 Cafes, Bars, and Street Food   66

CHAPTER 10: Nightlife and Entertainment   **70**

  10.1 Nightclubs and Bars   70
  10.2 Live Music and Performances   72
  10.3 Evening Cruises and Fireworks   75

CHAPTER 11: Shopping in Marmaris   **78**

  11.1 Local Markets and Handicrafts   78

    11.2 Modern Malls and Boutiques   81
    11.3 What to Buy: Souvenirs and Specialties   83

Chapter 12: Seasonal Highlights and Events   **86**
    12.1 Best Time to Visit Marmaris   86
    12.2 Festivals and Celebrations   88
    12.3 Seasonal Activities   90

Chapter 13: Practical Information for Travelers   **93**
    13.1 Currency and Payment Methods   93
    13.2 Local Customs and Etiquette   95
    13.3 Emergency Numbers and Safety Tips   97
    13.4 Language Tips and Useful Phrases   98

Chapter 14: Sustainability and Responsible Tourism101
    14.1 Supporting Local Businesses   101
    14.2 Eco-Friendly Activities   102
    14.3 Protecting Marmaris' Natural Beauty   104

Chapter 15: Planning Your Marmaris Itinerary   **107**
    15.1 Suggested 3-Day Itinerary   107
    15.2 One-Week Stay: A Balanced Adventure   109
    15.3 Long-Term Travel Tips   111

Chapter 16: FAQs and Traveler Insights   **115**
    16.1. Common Questions About Marmaris   115
    16.2. Tips from Experienced Visitors   117
    16.3. Resources for Further Reading   120

Chapter 1: Introduction to Marmaris

1.1 Welcome to Marmaris

Nestled along Turkey's stunning Turquoise Coast, Marmaris is a captivating seaside destination that seamlessly blends natural beauty, rich history, and vibrant modern life. Known for its crystalline waters, lush pine forests, and bustling marina, Marmaris attracts millions of visitors annually, offering something for everyone—from adventure seekers to leisure travelers.

As one of Turkey's most iconic coastal cities, Marmaris is a gateway to the Aegean and Mediterranean seas, offering breathtaking views and a unique fusion of cultures. Whether you're visiting for its sun-drenched beaches, lively nightlife, or historical treasures, Marmaris is a place where memories are made.

From the moment you arrive, you'll be struck by the welcoming atmosphere of Marmaris. Locals greet visitors with warm smiles, and the town's streets hum with the energy of people enjoying life's simple pleasures—sipping Turkish tea, bargaining in the bazaar, or sharing stories at waterfront cafes. Marmaris offers more than just a vacation; it's an invitation to experience the best of Turkey's coast in an environment that feels both luxurious and authentically Turkish.

Whether it's your first visit or one of many, Marmaris offers a sense of discovery that keeps you coming back for more. This travel guide will help you uncover the best of Marmaris, from its pristine beaches to its hidden gems.

1.2 Brief History of Marmaris

The roots of Marmaris stretch back thousands of years, giving this coastal gem a deep and intriguing history. The region is thought to have been settled as early as the 6th century BCE, originally known as *Physkos* in ancient Caria. Its strategic location at the crossroads of the Aegean and Mediterranean made it a significant hub for maritime trade and military campaigns throughout antiquity.

Marmaris has changed hands many times over the centuries, reflecting the rich tapestry of cultures that have left their mark here. It was ruled by the Carians, the

Persians, the Romans, and the Byzantines before eventually falling under Ottoman control in the 15th century. Each era brought new layers of history, leaving behind ruins, fortifications, and artifacts that hint at Marmaris' storied past.

A significant landmark in Marmaris is its castle, believed to have been built during the reign of Süleyman the Magnificent in 1522 when the Ottoman fleet launched its campaign against the Knights of Rhodes. The castle was later restored and now houses a museum showcasing archaeological finds and ethnographic exhibits.

In the 20th century, Marmaris was a small fishing village, relatively untouched by modern tourism. However, its natural beauty began to attract visitors in the 1980s, leading to its transformation into one of Turkey's premier tourist destinations. Despite this growth, Marmaris retains a connection to its heritage, with local traditions and historical sites serving as a reminder of its ancient origins.

1.3 Overview of Marmaris Today

Modern-day Marmaris is a vibrant, cosmopolitan town that has managed to balance its rich historical legacy with its role as a world-class tourist destination. Its pristine beaches stretch for miles, providing a paradise for sunseekers and water sports enthusiasts alike. The marina is one of the largest in Turkey, bustling with yachts and sailboats that give the town a cosmopolitan flair.

Marmaris is also a gateway to some of Turkey's most breathtaking natural attractions. Surrounding pine-covered hills provide a serene backdrop, while the nearby bays, islands, and coves are perfect for exploration by boat. The town's location makes it an ideal base for excursions to ancient ruins, charming villages, and natural wonders like Dalyan's mud baths or Cleopatra Island's golden sands.

The heart of Marmaris is its lively promenade, lined with restaurants, cafes, and shops. Here, visitors can enjoy a range of activities—from sampling fresh seafood to browsing for souvenirs in the Grand Bazaar. At night, Marmaris transforms into a hub of entertainment, with bars and clubs offering vibrant nightlife that lasts until dawn.

One of Marmaris' greatest strengths is its versatility. Families can enjoy safe, sandy beaches and kid-friendly attractions, while couples can escape to secluded coves or indulge in spa treatments at luxurious resorts. Adventure enthusiasts can go hiking, diving, or embark on thrilling jeep safaris through the surrounding countryside.

Despite its popularity, Marmaris has retained its charm and authenticity. The locals' warm hospitality, combined with the town's mix of history, culture, and natural beauty, ensures that every visitor feels at home. As Marmaris continues to grow and evolve, it remains a place where timeless traditions meet modern luxury, creating a destination that appeals to travelers from all walks of life.

Key Takeaways

Marmaris is more than just a beach town; it's a place where history, culture, and nature converge to create an unforgettable experience. Whether you're exploring ancient ruins, sailing through turquoise waters, or simply soaking up the sun, Marmaris offers a unique blend of relaxation and adventure. In the chapters ahead, we'll delve deeper into what makes Marmaris a must-visit destination and how to make the most of your time in this enchanting corner of Turkey.

Chapter 2: Getting to Marmaris

Marmaris, with its idyllic coastal charm and lush landscapes, is a destination that's easily accessible from various parts of the world. Whether you prefer the convenience of air travel, the scenic beauty of a road trip, or the adventure of arriving by sea, Marmaris offers a range of options to suit every traveler.

2.1 By Air: Nearest Airports and Transfers

For most international travelers, arriving in Marmaris by air is the quickest and most efficient option. Although Marmaris does not have its own airport, the town is served by two nearby international airports:

Dalaman Airport (DLM)
Located approximately 95 kilometers (59 miles) from

Marmaris, Dalaman Airport is the most popular choice for visitors. It is well-connected to major cities in Europe and the Middle East, with numerous seasonal flights catering to the tourist influx during the summer months. The airport offers modern facilities, including lounges, dining options, and duty-free shops.

Bodrum-Milas Airport (BJV)
Bodrum-Milas Airport is another option, located about 130 kilometers (81 miles) from Marmaris. While slightly farther away, it is an alternative for travelers who may not find suitable flights to Dalaman.

Transfers to Marmaris
Once you've landed at either airport, a variety of transfer options are available:

- **Private Transfers**: For comfort and convenience, many travelers opt for private transfers. These can be pre-booked and offer door-to-door service to your accommodation in Marmaris.
- **Shuttle Services**: Shared shuttle buses provide an affordable option and are commonly offered by tour operators and airport transfer companies.
- **Car Rentals**: Renting a car allows you the freedom to explore Marmaris and its surroundings at your own pace. Both Dalaman and Bodrum airports host a variety of car rental companies.
- **Taxis**: Taxis are readily available, but they can be expensive for the long journey. It's advisable to agree on a fare or ensure the meter is used.
- **Public Buses**: From Dalaman, you can take a short taxi ride to the local bus station (otogar)

and catch a bus to Marmaris. This is the most budget-friendly option, though it requires more time and effort.

2.2 By Road: Bus and Car Travel Options

Traveling to Marmaris by road offers the opportunity to enjoy Turkey's picturesque landscapes, with views ranging from rolling hills to the sparkling Aegean coastline. Whether you're coming from within Turkey or neighboring countries, Marmaris is well-connected by a network of highways.

By Bus
Turkey's intercity bus network is extensive, reliable, and affordable, making it a popular choice for domestic travelers. Several bus companies operate routes to Marmaris, with frequent services from major cities like Istanbul, Ankara, and Izmir.

- **Comfort and Amenities**: Turkish buses are known for their comfort, often equipped with air conditioning, onboard refreshments, and entertainment systems.
- **Arrival in Marmaris**: Buses arrive at the Marmaris Otogar (bus station), located a short distance from the town center. From there, taxis and local minibuses (*dolmuş*) are available to take you to your final destination.

By Car
Driving to Marmaris provides the ultimate flexibility and allows you to explore the scenic stops along the way.

- **Routes from Major Cities**:
    - From Istanbul: The journey is approximately 700 kilometers (435 miles) and takes about 9-10 hours by car. The route passes through Bursa and Izmir, both worth visiting.
    - From Ankara: Covering around 630 kilometers (391 miles), this drive takes about 8-9 hours. The route traverses the central Anatolian landscape, offering unique views.
    - From Izmir: A shorter drive of 260 kilometers (162 miles), taking about 4 hours, with a scenic coastal stretch near the end.
- **Car Rentals**: If you don't have your own vehicle, car rental services are widely available in major cities and airports.
- **Tips for Driving**: Turkish roads are generally in good condition, but be cautious on winding mountain roads near Marmaris. Ensure your vehicle is equipped with proper insurance and necessary documentation.

2.3 By Sea: Ferry and Cruise Routes

Arriving in Marmaris by sea is a memorable experience, offering stunning views of its turquoise waters and bustling marina. The town is a popular port of call for yachts, ferries, and cruise ships.

Ferry Services

- **From Rhodes, Greece**: One of the most popular ferry routes is between Marmaris and the island of Rhodes, Greece. High-speed catamarans operate daily during the tourist season, making it an excellent option for travelers exploring both Turkey and Greece. The journey takes approximately one hour.
- **Domestic Ferry Connections**: While Marmaris does not have extensive domestic ferry services, nearby ports like Bodrum and Fethiye offer connections to various Turkish coastal towns and islands.

Cruise Ships

Marmaris is a frequent stop for Mediterranean cruises, with its marina accommodating large vessels. Cruise passengers can spend a day exploring Marmaris' highlights before continuing their journey.

Private Yachts and Boats

For those seeking a more personalized experience, Marmaris is a hub for private yacht charters and sailing tours. Its location at the junction of the Aegean and Mediterranean seas makes it an ideal starting point for exploring Turkey's famous Blue Cruise routes.

Marina Facilities

Marmaris Marina is one of the largest and most modern in Turkey, offering world-class facilities for visiting boats and yachts. It's also a vibrant hub, surrounded by shops, restaurants, and cafes where sailors and travelers can relax.

Key Takeaways

Marmaris is accessible via air, road, and sea, making it a versatile destination for travelers worldwide. Whether you're flying into a nearby airport, driving through Turkey's scenic countryside, or arriving by ferry from a neighboring island, the journey to Marmaris is part of the adventure. Each mode of transportation offers unique perspectives, allowing you to begin your Marmaris experience even before you arrive. In the next chapters, we'll guide you through where to stay, what to explore, and how to make the most of your time in this stunning coastal town.

Chapter 3: Where to Stay in Marmaris

Marmaris offers a wide range of accommodation options that cater to different tastes, budgets, and travel styles. Whether you're seeking the opulence of a luxury resort, the charm of a budget-friendly guesthouse, the practicality of family-friendly lodgings, or the privacy of a villa, Marmaris has something to suit every traveler.

3.1 Luxury Resorts and Hotels

For those seeking indulgence and top-tier services, Marmaris is home to several luxurious resorts and hotels that promise a premium experience. Many of these accommodations are located along the coastline, offering stunning sea views, private beaches, and world-class amenities.

Top Features of Luxury Resorts

- **All-Inclusive Packages**: Many high-end resorts in Marmaris operate on an all-inclusive basis, providing guests with unlimited access to gourmet dining, beverages, and entertainment options.
- **Spa and Wellness**: Luxury hotels often feature lavish spa facilities offering traditional Turkish hammams, massages, and beauty treatments.
- **Private Beaches**: Some resorts have their own private stretches of beach, complete with sun loungers, cabanas, and attentive service.
- **Fine Dining**: On-site restaurants serve a mix of international and Turkish cuisines, often prepared by renowned chefs.
- **Activities and Entertainment**: From water sports to live music performances, luxury resorts go the extra mile to keep guests entertained.

Popular Luxury Stays in Marmaris

- **D-Resort Grand Azur**: Located in a prime waterfront position, this resort offers sleek

modern design, a lagoon-style pool, and direct beach access.
- **Elegance Hotels International**: Known for its sophisticated ambiance, this hotel features multiple dining options, a spa, and stunning sea views.
- **Marmaris Bay Resort**: Nestled amidst pine forests and overlooking a secluded bay, this adults-only resort is perfect for a tranquil getaway.

3.2 Budget-Friendly Accommodation

Travelers on a budget will find no shortage of affordable places to stay in Marmaris. Budget-friendly options include smaller hotels, family-run guesthouses, and hostels that provide comfort without breaking the bank.

Advantages of Budget Accommodation

- **Affordable Rates**: Enjoy clean and comfortable rooms at reasonable prices, often including breakfast.
- **Authentic Atmosphere**: Many smaller establishments are family-owned, offering a warm and personalized experience.
- **Central Locations**: Budget accommodations are often located close to Marmaris town center, making it easy to explore on foot.

Tips for Budget Travelers

- Book in advance, especially during peak tourist seasons, to secure the best deals.
- Look for package deals that include breakfast or discounts on local tours and activities.
- Consider staying slightly outside the town center, where prices may be lower, and transportation options are still convenient.

Popular Budget-Friendly Options

- **Blue Paradise Apart Hotel**: A cozy option with self-catering facilities and a swimming pool, ideal for travelers who want flexibility.
- **Hibiscus Garden Apart Hotel**: Affordable, family-friendly apartments with a relaxed vibe.
- **Karakas Apart Hotel**: Centrally located, offering comfortable rooms and friendly service.

3.3 Family-Friendly Stays

Marmaris is an excellent destination for families, and many accommodations cater specifically to those traveling with children. These family-friendly properties provide amenities and services designed to keep both kids and parents happy.

Family-Friendly Features

- **Kids' Clubs and Activities**: Many hotels have dedicated kids' clubs where children can enjoy games, crafts, and entertainment while parents relax.

- **Swimming Pools with Slides**: Family resorts often feature pools with water slides or separate kids' pools for safe swimming.
- **Spacious Rooms**: Family suites or interconnected rooms are designed to accommodate larger groups comfortably.
- **Childcare Services**: Babysitting and childcare facilities allow parents some time to unwind.

Recommended Family Stays

- **Green Nature Resort & Spa**: With its extensive activities for kids and adults alike, this resort is a family favorite.
- **Ideal Prime Beach Hotel**: Boasting beachfront access and a variety of pools, this hotel is perfect for families looking for convenience and fun.
- **Club Cettia Resort**: Offers family-friendly apartments with plenty of amenities and a lively atmosphere.

3.4 Alternative Lodgings: Villas and Apartments

For those seeking privacy and flexibility, villas and apartments are excellent alternatives to traditional hotels. These options are particularly appealing for families, groups of friends, or long-term travelers.

Advantages of Alternative Lodgings

- **Privacy and Space**: Villas offer private pools, gardens, and ample living space, making them ideal for a more secluded stay.
- **Self-Catering Facilities**: Apartments and villas typically come with fully equipped kitchens, allowing you to prepare your own meals.
- **Local Living Experience**: Staying in an apartment or villa provides an opportunity to immerse yourself in local life, shopping at local markets and cooking traditional Turkish dishes.

Popular Areas for Villas and Apartments

- **Içmeler**: A quieter area just outside Marmaris, known for its tranquil ambiance and beautiful surroundings.
- **Armutalan**: A residential neighborhood with a good selection of rental apartments and easy access to Marmaris town center.
- **Turunç**: A charming village south of Marmaris, offering a peaceful retreat with stunning views.

Popular Villas and Apartments

- **Villa Sun Apartments**: Budget-friendly apartments with a pool and close proximity to Marmaris' main attractions.
- **Grand Villa Sol Apart**: Spacious accommodations with a friendly atmosphere and modern amenities.
- **Turunç Holiday Villas**: Luxurious private villas set in a serene environment with breathtaking views.

Key Takeaways

Marmaris offers a diverse range of accommodations that cater to every traveler's needs, from lavish resorts and cozy budget stays to family-friendly hotels and private villas. Regardless of your choice, the town's warm hospitality and picturesque surroundings ensure a memorable stay. With your perfect base chosen, you'll be ready to explore all that Marmaris has to offer in the coming chapters.

Chapter 4: Exploring Marmaris Town

Marmaris is more than just a sun-soaked coastal destination; it's a vibrant town with a unique charm and rich history waiting to be explored. From its picturesque marina and historic landmarks to the bustling Grand Bazaar, Marmaris offers a wealth of experiences for travelers who want to dive into its culture, history, and everyday life.

4.1 Marmaris Marina and Promenade

The heart of Marmaris' social and leisure scene lies at its stunning marina and lively promenade. Known as one of the most beautiful marinas in Turkey, Marmaris Marina is a hub of activity where locals and tourists come together to enjoy the best of coastal life.

A Hub of Luxury and Leisure
 The marina is home to a fleet of luxury yachts, sailboats, and traditional Turkish gulets. As you stroll along the waterfront, you'll see vessels of all shapes and sizes, from modest fishing boats to opulent mega-yachts. This maritime diversity adds a touch of glamour and adventure to the marina's laid-back atmosphere.

Dining by the Sea
 The promenade that stretches along the marina is lined with cafes, restaurants, and bars offering stunning views of the bay. Dining here is a treat for all the senses. Whether you choose a fresh seafood platter, authentic Turkish kebabs, or international cuisine, you'll enjoy your meal with the gentle sound of waves lapping against the shore. Evening visitors are treated to the sight of the marina bathed in soft lights, creating a romantic and serene ambiance.

Shopping and Entertainment

The marina area also features boutique shops selling everything from designer clothing to handmade souvenirs. In the evening, the marina comes alive with live music and cultural performances, making it an ideal spot for a relaxing yet lively night out.

A Gateway to Adventure

Marmaris Marina isn't just a place to relax; it's also the starting point for many adventures. From here, you can embark on daily boat tours, fishing trips, or private yacht charters to explore nearby islands, hidden coves, and the turquoise waters of the Aegean.

Must-See Highlights Along the Promenade

- **Statue of Mustafa Kemal Atatürk**: A tribute to Turkey's founding father, this statue is a popular photo spot.
- **Fountains and Green Spaces**: Perfect for a leisurely walk or a quiet moment to enjoy the scenery.
- **Sunset Views**: The promenade offers some of the best spots to watch the sun dip below the horizon.

4.2 Marmaris Castle and Museum

Perched on a hill overlooking the marina, Marmaris Castle is one of the town's most iconic landmarks. This historic fortress is a must-visit for anyone interested in the town's rich history and breathtaking views.

A Fortress with a Story
The origins of Marmaris Castle date back to 3000 BCE, but the structure we see today was significantly rebuilt during the reign of Ottoman Sultan Süleyman the Magnificent in 1522. The castle served as a strategic base during the Ottoman campaign against the Knights of Rhodes.

Exploring the Castle
The castle is remarkably well-preserved and offers a fascinating glimpse into the past. Visitors can wander through its ancient walls, explore its courtyards, and imagine the battles that once took place here. The elevated position of the castle provides panoramic views of Marmaris Bay, the marina, and the surrounding hills—a photographer's dream.

The Museum Inside
Marmaris Castle is also home to a small but engaging museum showcasing the region's archaeological and ethnographic history.

- **Archaeological Exhibits**: Artifacts from the ancient Carian and Hellenistic periods, including pottery, coins, and tools, highlight the area's rich heritage.
- **Ethnographic Displays**: Exhibits featuring traditional Turkish household items, textiles, and costumes provide insight into the region's cultural history.
- **Interactive Features**: Some sections of the museum offer hands-on displays or detailed explanations, making it accessible for all ages.

Practical Tips for Visiting

- **Opening Hours**: The castle is open daily, though hours may vary seasonally.
- **Admission Fee**: Entry is reasonably priced, with discounts for students and children.
- **What to Bring**: Comfortable shoes are a must, as the castle involves climbing stairs and navigating uneven surfaces.

A Link to the Past

Visiting Marmaris Castle is a reminder of the town's historical significance and its enduring connection to the sea. It's a quiet retreat from the hustle and bustle of the town below and a space where history truly comes alive.

4.3 Grand Bazaar: Local Shopping Experience

No visit to Marmaris is complete without a trip to its Grand Bazaar, a vibrant marketplace brimming with sights, sounds, and aromas. Known locally as the *Kapalı Çarşı*, the Grand Bazaar is a treasure trove of goods that reflects the town's unique blend of traditional and modern influences.

A Shopper's Paradise

The Grand Bazaar consists of a labyrinth of covered streets lined with hundreds of shops selling everything from clothing and jewelry to spices and souvenirs. Whether you're a seasoned haggler or a casual browser, the bazaar offers an unforgettable shopping experience.

What to Buy

- **Turkish Textiles**: From handwoven carpets to colorful scarves, Turkish textiles are renowned for their quality and craftsmanship.
- **Spices and Teas**: The bazaar's spice shops are a feast for the senses, offering exotic blends, herbal teas, and Turkish coffee.
- **Gold and Silver Jewelry**: Marmaris is famous for its intricately designed jewelry, available at competitive prices.
- **Leather Goods**: Bags, jackets, and belts made from high-quality leather are popular purchases.
- **Souvenirs**: Handmade ceramics, evil eye charms, and miniature gulet boats make for meaningful keepsakes.

Tips for Navigating the Bazaar

- **Haggling is Expected**: Bargaining is a common practice, so don't be afraid to negotiate for a better price.
- **Cash is King**: While many shops accept credit cards, smaller vendors often prefer cash.
- **Stay Hydrated**: Exploring the bazaar can be an energetic activity, so take breaks and enjoy a refreshing glass of Turkish tea.

Beyond Shopping

The Grand Bazaar isn't just a place to shop; it's a cultural experience. The friendly banter of shopkeepers, the rich aroma of spices, and the colorful displays create an atmosphere that's quintessentially Turkish. Take your time to soak it all in and perhaps strike up a conversation with the locals—they often have fascinating stories to share.

Key Takeaways

Marmaris Town is a dynamic mix of history, culture, and modern vibrancy. From the scenic charm of the marina and promenade to the historical significance of Marmaris Castle and the bustling energy of the Grand Bazaar, there's something for everyone to enjoy. Exploring these highlights offers a deeper appreciation of Marmaris' unique character and its enduring appeal as a top travel destination. In the next chapters, we'll dive into the beaches, outdoor adventures, and day trips that make Marmaris a true paradise for travelers.

Chapter 5: Beaches and Waterfront Activities

Marmaris, with its stunning coastline and crystal-clear waters, is a paradise for beach lovers and water enthusiasts. The town boasts a variety of beaches, from lively stretches with vibrant atmospheres to tranquil coves ideal for relaxation. Alongside its beaches, Marmaris offers a plethora of waterfront activities, making it a haven for both thrill-seekers and those looking for a serene retreat.

5.1 Best Beaches in Marmaris

Marmaris is blessed with some of the most picturesque beaches on Turkey's Turquoise Coast. Each beach has its own character, offering something unique for every type of traveler.

1. Marmaris Public Beach

Located near the town center, Marmaris Public Beach is the most accessible and popular beach in the area.

- **Vibe**: Lively and energetic, perfect for socializing and people-watching.
- **Amenities**: Sun loungers, umbrellas, beachfront cafes, and restaurants line the shore.
- **Activities**: Ideal for swimming, beach volleyball, and casual strolls along the promenade.

2. Içmeler Beach

Just a short drive from Marmaris, Içmeler Beach is known for its calm waters and family-friendly atmosphere.

- **Vibe**: Relaxed and peaceful, making it great for families with children.
- **Amenities**: Well-maintained facilities, including changing rooms, showers, and rental sunbeds.
- **Activities**: Paddleboarding, snorkeling, and pedal boating are popular here.

3. Turunç Beach

Nestled in a charming village, Turunç Beach is a Blue Flag beach that boasts pristine waters and a more secluded feel.

- **Vibe**: Tranquil and picturesque, ideal for a quiet escape.
- **Amenities**: A handful of local cafes and restaurants, along with sunbeds and umbrellas.
- **Activities**: Perfect for snorkeling and enjoying the natural beauty of the surrounding hills.

4. Cleopatra Island (Sedir Island)

For a truly unique experience, take a boat trip to Cleopatra Island, famed for its soft, golden sands said to have been imported from Egypt.

- **Vibe**: Exotic and historical, steeped in legend and natural beauty.
- **Amenities**: Basic facilities and designated areas for swimming and lounging.

- **Activities**: Explore ancient ruins, swim in clear waters, or marvel at the unique sand texture.

5. Kumlubük Beach

Situated in a serene bay, Kumlubük Beach is less crowded and offers a tranquil retreat for those looking to escape the bustle of Marmaris.

- **Vibe**: Undisturbed and scenic, ideal for couples or solo travelers.
- **Amenities**: Limited facilities, but a few restaurants nearby serve fresh seafood.
- **Activities**: Hiking trails in the area lead to breathtaking viewpoints.

5.2 Water Sports: Jet Skiing, Parasailing, and More

For those who thrive on adrenaline, Marmaris offers an array of water sports that make full use of its beautiful coastal setting. Whether you're a novice or an experienced adventurer, there's something for everyone.

1. Jet Skiing

Feel the thrill of speeding across the waves on a jet ski. Marmaris' calm and clear waters make it a perfect location for this exhilarating activity.

- **Where**: Available at most major beaches, including Marmaris Public Beach and Içmeler Beach.

- **Tips**: Beginners can opt for guided sessions to learn the basics, while experienced riders can explore freely.

2. Parasailing
Get a bird's-eye view of Marmaris as you soar above the sea with parasailing.

- **Experience**: The combination of breathtaking aerial views and the adrenaline rush of being high above the water is unforgettable.
- **Safety**: Professional operators ensure you're equipped with secure harnesses and provide detailed instructions.

3. Scuba Diving
Marmaris' underwater world is just as mesmerizing as its coastline. Explore coral reefs, underwater caves, and vibrant marine life.

- **Dive Spots**: Popular locations include Baca Cave and Aquarium Bay.
- **For Beginners**: Many diving schools in Marmaris offer introductory dives with certified instructors.

4. Banana Boating and Ringo Rides
For families or groups, banana boats and ringo rides provide a fun and laughter-filled experience.

- **What to Expect**: Hold on tight as a speedboat pulls you along the water on an inflatable banana or ring-shaped raft.

- **Who It's For**: These activities are suitable for all ages and require no prior experience.

5. Stand-Up Paddleboarding and Kayaking
For a more relaxed water activity, try stand-up paddleboarding (SUP) or kayaking.

- **Ideal Locations**: The calm waters of Içmeler Beach and Turunç Beach are perfect for these activities.
- **Why It's Great**: Paddleboarding and kayaking offer a workout while allowing you to soak in the stunning scenery.

5.3 Relaxing Beach Clubs

For those who want to combine luxury and leisure, Marmaris' beach clubs offer the ultimate in comfort and style. These exclusive spots provide a blend of sun, sea, and sophisticated amenities.

1. Nirvana Beach Club
Located on the Marmaris promenade, Nirvana Beach Club is known for its chic vibe and exceptional service.

- **Highlights**: Comfortable loungers, a well-stocked bar, and live DJ performances in the evening.
- **Food and Drinks**: Enjoy gourmet dishes and signature cocktails while soaking up the sun.

2. Içmeler Beach Club
This family-friendly beach club is a favorite among visitors to Içmeler Beach.

- **Highlights**: Shaded cabanas, shallow swimming areas, and activities for kids.
- **Why It's Unique**: A laid-back ambiance with attentive staff ensures a relaxing day by the sea.

3. Blue Port Beach Club
Situated near the marina, Blue Port Beach Club offers a modern and lively atmosphere.

- **Highlights**: A stylish infinity pool, sun terraces, and direct beach access.
- **For Night Owls**: The club transforms into a vibrant nightlife venue after sunset.

4. Bonjuk Bay
For a more secluded and eco-conscious option, Bonjuk Bay is a hidden gem located a short drive from Marmaris.

- **Highlights**: A focus on sustainability, with organic food options and eco-friendly practices.
- **Perfect For**: Yoga enthusiasts, artists, and those seeking a retreat from the crowds.

5. Maris Beach Club
A classic choice along Marmaris Public Beach, Maris Beach Club offers a perfect mix of relaxation and entertainment.

- **Highlights**: Regular live music, themed parties, and a menu featuring local and international dishes.
- **Why It Stands Out**: Its central location makes it a convenient choice for travelers staying in the town center.

Key Takeaways

Marmaris' beaches and waterfront activities are integral to its allure, offering everything from sunbathing and swimming to thrilling water sports and upscale beach club experiences. Whether you're seeking adventure, family fun, or a tranquil escape, the diverse coastal offerings ensure that every visitor can craft their perfect seaside getaway. In the next chapters, we'll explore Marmaris' rich natural surroundings and cultural excursions, so you can continue uncovering the treasures of this coastal paradise.

Chapter 6: Day Trips and Excursions

While Marmaris itself is a treasure trove of attractions and activities, its surrounding areas offer equally enticing experiences. A variety of day trips and excursions allow visitors to delve into the region's natural beauty, historical landmarks, and cultural richness. Whether you're exploring Cleopatra Island's legendary sands, gliding along the Dalyan River, or immersing yourself in traditional Turkish village life, these excursions promise unforgettable memories.

6.1 Cleopatra Island (Sedir Island)

Cleopatra Island, also known as Sedir Island, is a captivating destination just a short boat ride from Marmaris. Renowned for its golden sand and stunning scenery, this island is steeped in legend and natural beauty.

The Legend of Cleopatra's Sand
According to local lore, Cleopatra and her lover Mark Antony once visited this island. To ensure the queen's comfort, Mark Antony had sand imported all the way

from Egypt. The sand's unique texture and composition—consisting of spherical grains not found elsewhere in Turkey—support this legend, adding a romantic and mysterious allure to the island.

Exploring Cleopatra Island

- **Golden Beach**: The main attraction is the beach, which features the fabled golden sand. Swimming here feels like a dream, with the crystal-clear waters and the unique softness of the sand beneath your feet. Note that the beach is protected, and visitors are not allowed to remove any sand.
- **Ancient Ruins**: Beyond its beach, the island is home to the remnants of an ancient Roman settlement. Explore the ruins of a Roman amphitheater and temples, which provide a glimpse into the island's historical significance.
- **Natural Beauty**: The island is also known for its lush greenery and panoramic views of the surrounding Aegean Sea, making it a perfect spot for nature lovers and photographers.

Getting There

Boat trips to Cleopatra Island depart regularly from Marmaris and nearby towns such as Çamlı. Many tours include lunch and a guided exploration of the island, making it a hassle-free day trip.

6.2 Dalyan River Cruise and Mud Baths

A day trip to the Dalyan River offers a perfect blend of natural beauty, relaxation, and history. This excursion is a favorite among visitors looking to experience the diverse attractions of the region.

The Dalyan River
The Dalyan River meanders through a picturesque landscape of reed beds and wetlands. A boat cruise along this river is a serene and scenic journey that showcases the region's ecological diversity.

Kaunos Tombs
One of the highlights of the Dalyan River cruise is the sight of the Lycian rock tombs carved into the cliffs. These tombs, part of the ancient city of Kaunos, date back to the 4th century BCE and are a remarkable example of Lycian craftsmanship and funerary architecture.

- **Photography Tip**: Early morning or late afternoon light makes for stunning photographs of the tombs.
- **Cultural Insight**: Guides often share fascinating stories about the tombs and the ancient Lycian civilization.

Iztuzu Beach (Turtle Beach)
The Dalyan River flows into Iztuzu Beach, a protected

nesting site for the endangered loggerhead sea turtles (*Caretta caretta*).

- **What to Do**: Visitors can relax on the sandy beach, swim in the clear waters, or observe conservation efforts at the nearby turtle rehabilitation center.
- **Eco-Friendly Tourism**: The beach is a designated conservation area, so visitor activities are carefully managed to protect the turtles and their habitat.

The Famous Mud Baths

The mud baths of Dalyan are both a fun and rejuvenating experience.

- **How It Works**: Visitors slather themselves in nutrient-rich mud, allow it to dry, and then rinse off in a nearby thermal spring. The mud is said to have detoxifying and skin-rejuvenating properties.
- **Fun for All**: This activity is enjoyable for people of all ages, and the atmosphere is light-hearted and communal.
- **Practical Tip**: Wear a swimsuit you don't mind getting muddy, and bring a towel and change of clothes.

Getting There

Daily tours to Dalyan River often include transportation, meals, and guided activities, making it a convenient and comprehensive excursion from Marmaris.

6.3 Village Tours: Traditional Turkish Life

For travelers seeking a deeper connection with Turkish culture and traditions, a village tour offers an enriching experience. These tours take you away from the hustle and bustle of Marmaris to the serene countryside, where time seems to stand still.

Visiting Bayır Village
One of the most popular village stops is Bayır, located in the verdant hills near Marmaris.

- **Famous for Honey**: Bayır is known for its production of pine honey, a local delicacy. Visitors can sample and purchase this sweet treat from village vendors.
- **Ancient Plane Tree**: The village square is home to a centuries-old plane tree, believed to bring good luck to those who circle it.
- **Village Life**: Strolling through the narrow streets, you'll see traditional stone houses, small farms, and local artisans at work.

Exploring Turgut Village
Another must-visit is Turgut Village, known for its handicrafts and warm hospitality.

- **Handmade Rugs**: Turgut is famous for its intricately woven rugs, each telling a story through its patterns and colors. You can watch artisans at work and even try weaving on a loom.

- **Waterfall Trek**: A short hike from the village leads to a beautiful waterfall, a perfect spot for a refreshing dip or a picnic.

Cooking and Craft Workshops

Many village tours include hands-on experiences such as cooking traditional Turkish dishes or learning to make handicrafts.

- **Cooking Classes**: Learn to prepare iconic dishes like *dolma* (stuffed grape leaves) or *gözleme* (Turkish flatbread).
- **Pottery and Weaving**: Try your hand at creating pottery or weaving baskets using traditional techniques.

Local Hospitality

One of the most memorable aspects of a village tour is the genuine warmth and hospitality of the villagers. Many tours include a traditional Turkish lunch, served in a family home or a local eatery, where you can savor authentic flavors and engage in heartfelt conversations.

Key Takeaways

Day trips and excursions from Marmaris provide an incredible opportunity to experience the natural beauty, history, and culture of the surrounding region. Whether you're lounging on Cleopatra Island's legendary sands, exploring the ecological wonders of the Dalyan River, or immersing yourself in the rhythms of village life, these experiences add depth and diversity to your Marmaris adventure. As we move to the next chapters, we'll explore Marmaris' nightlife, gastronomy, and outdoor adventures to round out your travel itinerary.

CHAPTER 7: Outdoor Adventures

Nestled between the turquoise waters of the Aegean Sea and the verdant hills of Turkey's southwestern coast, Marmaris is a haven for outdoor enthusiasts. Its diverse landscape offers activities that combine natural beauty, adventure, and a touch of cultural exploration. Whether you're a seasoned adventurer or a nature lover looking for tranquility, Marmaris promises unforgettable experiences. Let's delve into three captivating outdoor activities that you must explore in this stunning destination.

7.1 Hiking Trails and Nature Walks

The Call of the Wild in Marmaris

Marmaris is a paradise for hikers and nature walkers, with its picturesque trails weaving through lush pine forests, rugged mountain terrain, and breathtaking coastal vistas. The region's trails cater to various difficulty levels, ensuring both beginners and seasoned hikers can find a route that suits their pace. Here's why hiking in Marmaris should be on your bucket list:

Popular Hiking Trails

1. **Marmaris National Park**: This park is a treasure trove of biodiversity. You'll traverse paths surrounded by towering pine trees, wildflowers, and the occasional glimpse of wildlife like deer or squirrels. The air here is intoxicatingly fresh, making every step a delight.
2. **Kızkumu (Maiden's Sand)**: Located near Orhaniye, this trail combines a gentle hike with an iconic walk across a submerged sandbar that stretches into the sea. It's a blend of natural wonder and cultural legend, as local lore ties the area to a romantic tale.
3. **Bozburun Peninsula Trails**: For the adventurous, this peninsula offers a mix of coastal and inland routes. Hikers can enjoy panoramic views of the Aegean, ancient ruins, and sleepy fishing villages.

Key Highlights

- **Historical Insights**: Many trails lead to ancient ruins, including Lycian tombs, crumbling

fortresses, and remnants of old trade routes, offering a blend of exercise and education.
- **Seasonal Delights**: Spring brings blooming wildflowers, while autumn offers cooler weather and colorful foliage, making these seasons the ideal times to hike.
- **Guided Tours**: Local guides provide rich narratives about the flora, fauna, and history of the area, making the experience even more enriching.

Tips for Hiking in Marmaris

- Always carry water, sunscreen, and sturdy footwear.
- Start early to avoid the midday heat, especially in summer.
- Respect the environment by not littering and staying on designated paths.

Conclusion: Hiking in Marmaris is not just about reaching a destination—it's about soaking in the journey. Each trail tells a story, and the natural beauty leaves you with memories that last a lifetime.

7.2 Off-Road Safari Experiences

An Adrenaline-Packed Journey

For those who crave adventure beyond conventional sightseeing, off-road safari experiences in Marmaris offer an exhilarating escape. Riding through rugged landscapes in open-top jeeps, you'll explore hidden corners of the region that most tourists never see. It's an opportunity to get your adrenaline pumping while uncovering Marmaris' untamed beauty.

What to Expect

- **Thrilling Terrain**: Safari routes take you through bumpy forest trails, rocky mountain paths, and shallow riverbeds, making for an exciting ride. Expect plenty of twists, turns, and splashes!
- **Scenic Stops**: Along the way, you'll stop at picturesque spots like Turgut Falls, where you can take a refreshing dip, or secluded beaches perfect for a picnic.
- **Local Encounters**: Safaris often include visits to traditional Turkish villages, giving you a glimpse into local life. Meet friendly villagers, sample homemade honey, or sip on fresh pomegranate juice.

Top Safari Experiences

1. **Marmaris Jeep Safari**: One of the most popular options, this tour combines off-roading with stops at iconic sites like the Jesus Beach and the cascading waterfalls of Turgut.
2. **Dalyan Mud Safari**: This adventure adds a twist with stops at thermal mud baths and a cruise down the Dalyan River to view the famous Lycian Rock Tombs.

Why Go Off-Roading?

- **Family-Friendly Fun**: Safaris are great for families, as they're thrilling yet safe, and kids love the excitement of bouncing along the trails.

- **Photography Opportunities**: The vistas you'll encounter are postcard-perfect. From dramatic mountain views to serene countryside scenes, you'll have endless moments to capture.
- **Connection to Nature**: This adventure takes you off the beaten path, immersing you in the raw beauty of Marmaris away from bustling tourist areas.

Preparation Tips

- Wear comfortable, weather-appropriate clothing.
- Pack essentials like sunglasses, a hat, and a scarf to protect against dust.
- Bring a waterproof camera or phone case to capture the fun.

Conclusion: Off-road safaris in Marmaris are more than just an activity—they're a journey into the heart of this captivating region. The combination of adventure, nature, and culture makes it an unmissable experience.

7.3 Cycling Around Marmaris

Two Wheels, Endless Exploration

Cycling is one of the most rewarding ways to explore Marmaris. With its mix of scenic coastal roads, forested trails, and charming villages, the area offers cycling routes for all skill levels. Whether you're a casual rider looking for a relaxing ride or an avid cyclist seeking a challenge, Marmaris delivers.

Best Cycling Routes

1. **Marmaris to İçmeler**: This is a favorite among visitors for its stunning coastal views. The path is well-paved and relatively flat, making it ideal for beginners or families.
2. **Bozburun Peninsula Circuit**: Advanced cyclists will love this longer route that takes you through picturesque villages, rugged hills, and serene beaches. The climbs are worth it for the panoramic views.
3. **Gökova Gulf Ride**: A scenic trail that combines coastal roads with glimpses of lush greenery and traditional Turkish settlements.

Cycling Highlights

- **Customizable Experience**: Rent a bike and explore at your own pace or join a guided tour for a more structured adventure.
- **Eco-Friendly Travel**: Cycling allows you to immerse yourself in nature while leaving a minimal environmental footprint.
- **Healthy and Fun**: Not only is cycling a great workout, but it also offers a unique perspective on Marmaris that you can't get from a car or bus.

Cycling Events

Marmaris often hosts cycling festivals and competitions, attracting riders from around the world. Participating in or watching these events can add an extra layer of excitement to your visit.

Tips for Cyclists

- Ensure your bike is in good condition and carry basic repair tools.
- Stick to designated cycling paths for safety.
- Hydrate regularly, especially in the warmer months.

Conclusion: Cycling around Marmaris is a liberating way to experience its natural and cultural riches. Every turn of the wheel reveals a new wonder, making it an adventure you'll cherish.

Marmaris' outdoor adventures offer something for everyone, from serene hikes to adrenaline-fueled safaris and leisurely cycling routes. Each activity provides a unique way to connect with the area's stunning landscapes and rich culture. So lace up your boots, hop on a bike, or buckle up for a wild ride—Marmaris is waiting to be explored!

CHAPTER 8: Cultural and Historical Landmarks

Marmaris is more than just a sun-soaked paradise with shimmering seas and lush forests; it is also a region steeped in culture and history. Its vibrant past, shaped by the influences of ancient civilizations, Ottoman rule, and local traditions, can be explored through its array of cultural and historical landmarks. From ancient ruins to sacred mosques and traditional Turkish baths, Marmaris invites visitors to dive into its rich heritage. Let's explore these remarkable highlights.

8.1 Ancient Ruins Near Marmaris

A Journey Back in Time

Marmaris is surrounded by remnants of ancient civilizations that once thrived in this region, including the Greeks, Romans, and Byzantines. These archaeological sites tell fascinating stories of trade, conquest, and daily life in antiquity, making them a must-visit for history buffs and curious travelers alike.

Key Ancient Sites

1. **Kaunos**
   Located near Dalyan, Kaunos is one of the most impressive ancient cities near Marmaris. The site features rock-cut Lycian tombs carved into cliffs, a theater with sweeping views of the surrounding countryside, and remains of temples and baths. The serenity of the area, combined with its historical significance, creates an unforgettable experience.
   - **Highlights**: Lycian Rock Tombs, Acropolis, and the Harbor Agora.
   - **Tip**: Take a boat ride along the Dalyan River for a scenic approach to Kaunos.
2. **Knidos**
   Situated on the Datça Peninsula, Knidos was a

prominent city of ancient Caria, renowned for its advancements in science, art, and medicine. Its most famous feature is the Temple of Aphrodite, which once housed a celebrated statue by the sculptor Praxiteles. Visitors can also explore the amphitheater, ancient harbor, and remnants of residential areas.
- **Highlights**: Temple of Aphrodite, twin harbors, and the Hellenistic theater.
- **Tip**: Visit during sunset to witness breathtaking views over the Aegean Sea.

3. **Amos**

Closer to Marmaris, the ancient city of Amos offers a less crowded but equally fascinating glimpse into history. Perched on a hill overlooking the sea, Amos is known for its well-preserved amphitheater, city walls, and remnants of temples.
- **Highlights**: Amphitheater and panoramic views of Turunç Bay.
- **Tip**: Pair your visit with a hike in the surrounding hills for a nature-infused historical adventure.

Why Visit These Ruins?

- They provide insight into ancient architectural techniques and urban planning.
- They allow visitors to connect with the stories of the past in a tangible way.

- They are often located in scenic, peaceful settings, combining natural beauty with historical exploration.

8.2 Local Mosques and Religious Sites

Sacred Spaces of Marmaris

Marmaris' mosques and religious sites reflect its Ottoman heritage and serve as peaceful sanctuaries where visitors can admire traditional Islamic architecture and experience the spiritual heartbeat of the region. These landmarks are not just places of worship but also bear witness to the community's cultural identity.

Notable Mosques

1. **İbrahim Ağa Mosque**
   This 18th-century mosque, located in the heart of Marmaris, is an architectural gem. With its modest yet elegant design, it features a single minaret and intricate tile work inside. Visitors can observe the harmonious blend of simplicity and beauty characteristic of Ottoman-era mosques.
   - **Highlights**: Ottoman architecture, serene courtyard, and historical significance.
   - **Tip**: Visit during off-peak hours to enjoy the tranquility.
2. **Kemerli Mosque (Tashan Mosque)**
   Located in the nearby town of Muğla, this

mosque is a standout for its unique stone construction and charming arched entrances. It is a beautiful example of how Islamic architectural principles were adapted to local materials and styles.
    - **Highlights**: Stone arches and historical ambiance.
    - **Tip**: Pair your visit with a walk through Muğla's old town for a cultural immersion.
3. **Sedir Island Chapel**
    Though not a mosque, this small Byzantine chapel on Sedir Island is worth mentioning for its spiritual significance and historical allure. The island itself, often associated with Cleopatra's Beach, offers an intriguing mix of natural beauty and historical depth.
    - **Highlights**: Frescoes and panoramic island views.
    - **Tip**: Combine your visit with a swim at Cleopatra Beach for a perfect day out.

Why Visit Religious Sites?

- They offer a serene escape from the bustling tourist areas.
- They provide a deeper understanding of local religious and cultural practices.
- They showcase architectural styles that are both functional and artistic.

Respecting Local Customs

When visiting mosques, it's essential to dress modestly, covering shoulders and knees, and remove your shoes before entering. Women may be required to cover their hair with a scarf, which is often provided at the entrance.

8.3 Traditional Turkish Baths

A Timeless Wellness Tradition

No visit to Marmaris is complete without experiencing a traditional Turkish bath, or *hamam*. This centuries-old practice is not only a ritual of cleansing but also a cornerstone of Turkish culture, symbolizing relaxation, rejuvenation, and hospitality.

What to Expect in a Turkish Bath

- **Warm-Up Stage**: Begin in the *hararet* (hot room), a heated marble chamber designed to make you sweat and open your pores. The ambient warmth is soothing and prepares your body for the cleansing process.
- **Exfoliation**: A professional attendant will use a coarse mitt, known as a *kese*, to scrub away dead skin, leaving your skin silky smooth.
- **Foam Massage**: Next comes the foam massage, where you'll be enveloped in a cloud of soapy bubbles while enjoying a gentle yet invigorating massage.
- **Rinse and Relax**: Finally, rinse off with cool water and unwind in the lounge area with a cup of Turkish tea.

Popular Turkish Baths in Marmaris

1. **Armutalan Turkish Bath**
   One of the most popular *hamams* in Marmaris, Armutalan offers a range of packages that include exfoliation, massages, and facials. Its authentic ambiance and skilled staff ensure a memorable experience.
   - **Highlights**: Affordable packages and a welcoming atmosphere.
   - **Tip**: Book your session early in your trip to relax after travel and prepare your skin for sunbathing.
2. **Grand Bazzar Turkish Bath**
   Located near Marmaris' bustling bazaar, this *hamam* combines traditional techniques with modern amenities. It's a convenient option for travelers exploring the town center.
   - **Highlights**: Central location and combination treatments.
   - **Tip**: Pair your bath with a shopping spree in the bazaar.
3. **Dalyan Mud Baths**
   While not a traditional *hamam*, the mud baths near Dalyan offer a similar cleansing and rejuvenating experience. Visitors cover themselves in therapeutic mud, let it dry, and rinse off in mineral-rich thermal waters.
   - **Highlights**: Therapeutic benefits and a fun, communal vibe.
   - **Tip**: Wear an older swimsuit as the mud can stain fabrics.

Health Benefits of Turkish Baths

- Promotes better blood circulation.
- Exfoliates and cleanses the skin deeply.
- Relieves stress and muscle tension.

Conclusion

From the echoes of ancient civilizations to the serene prayers in local mosques and the age-old ritual of the Turkish bath, Marmaris offers a diverse tapestry of cultural and historical experiences. Exploring these landmarks allows visitors to connect with the soul of the region, gaining insights into its vibrant past and enduring traditions. Whether you're walking among the ruins, marveling at Islamic architecture, or indulging in a relaxing *hamam*, Marmaris promises a journey of discovery that stays with you long after you leave.

CHAPTER 9: Dining in Marmaris

Marmaris is not just a feast for the eyes with its stunning beaches and lush mountains—it's also a paradise for food lovers. The town's culinary scene combines traditional Turkish flavors, fresh seafood, and international influences, offering something for every palate. Dining in Marmaris isn't just about eating; it's about immersing yourself in the culture and savoring the hospitality that Turkey is known for. Let's embark on a delicious journey through the best dining experiences Marmaris has to offer.

9.1 Authentic Turkish Cuisine

A Symphony of Flavors

Turkish cuisine is a rich mosaic of flavors, shaped by centuries of diverse cultural influences. In Marmaris, you'll find restaurants and eateries offering dishes that highlight the essence of this heritage. Whether it's a hearty stew, freshly baked bread, or a sweet treat, every bite tells a story.

Must-Try Turkish Dishes in Marmaris

1. **Meze**
   Start your meal with a selection of *meze*, small plates that include classics like *hummus*, *haydari* (yogurt with garlic and dill), *ezme* (spicy tomato salad), and stuffed grape leaves (*yaprak sarma*). These are usually served with warm *pide* bread.
   - **Tip**: Pair your *meze* with a glass of *rakı*, Turkey's beloved anise-flavored spirit.
2. **Kebabs**
   Turkish kebabs are a staple, and Marmaris serves them in all their glory. Try the succulent

Adana kebab, spiced minced meat grilled on skewers, or *Iskender kebab*, slices of lamb served with tomato sauce and yogurt.
    - **Tip**: Look for restaurants with charcoal grills for the most authentic flavor.
3. **Gözleme**
    This traditional Turkish flatbread is stuffed with fillings like spinach, cheese, or minced meat and cooked on a griddle. It's a simple yet satisfying dish often found in local markets or roadside eateries.
    - **Tip**: Enjoy it fresh with a side of homemade yogurt.
4. **Mantı**
    Turkish dumplings filled with minced meat and topped with garlic yogurt and paprika-infused butter are a must-try for those who love comfort food.
    - **Tip**: Smaller, hand-crafted *mantı* are considered superior.
5. **Baklava and Turkish Delight**
    End your meal on a sweet note with flaky, syrupy *baklava* or sample an assortment of chewy Turkish delight (*lokum*). Both pair perfectly with a cup of Turkish coffee.
    - **Tip**: Visit a local patisserie for the freshest options.

Dining Experiences

- **Family-Owned Taverns**: Many of Marmaris' best Turkish meals come from family-owned

establishments where recipes are passed down through generations.
- **Turkish Breakfast**: Don't miss a traditional Turkish breakfast (*kahvaltı*), featuring olives, cheeses, eggs, honey, and endless tea refills. Some restaurants offer breathtaking views to accompany this feast.

Conclusion: Authentic Turkish cuisine in Marmaris is not just about nourishment—it's about experiencing a way of life. The warmth of the food reflects the hospitality of the people, making every meal unforgettable.

9.2 Seafood Restaurants by the Coast

From Sea to Plate

With its prime location along the Aegean coast, Marmaris is renowned for its fresh and flavorful seafood. Dining by the coast is an experience that combines the taste of the ocean with stunning views, as you enjoy meals prepared with the day's freshest catch.

Popular Seafood Dishes

1. **Grilled Sea Bream (Çupra)**
   A staple on most seafood menus, this tender fish is simply seasoned and grilled to perfection.
   - **Tip**: Ask for a drizzle of olive oil and lemon for added flavor.

2. **Octopus Salad**
   Fresh, tender octopus mixed with olive oil, lemon, and herbs makes for a refreshing appetizer.
   - **Tip**: Pair it with a crisp white wine for a complete experience.
3. **Stuffed Mussels (Midye Dolma)**
   These delicious bites consist of mussels stuffed with spiced rice and served with a squeeze of lemon.
   - **Tip**: Often sold by street vendors, they're a perfect on-the-go snack.
4. **Lobster and King Prawns**
   For a luxurious treat, indulge in freshly caught lobster or jumbo prawns, often grilled or served in a rich garlic butter sauce.
   - **Tip**: Pre-order these at select seafood restaurants for guaranteed availability.
5. **Calamari (Kalamar)**
   Lightly fried calamari rings are a crowd favorite. They're crispy on the outside and tender on the inside, served with a tangy dipping sauce.
   - **Tip**: Look for restaurants that serve freshly made sauces, as they enhance the dish.

Top Coastal Restaurants

1. **Dede Restaurant**
   Located in Marmaris Marina, Dede is known for its spectacular seafood platters and romantic

ambiance. Diners can enjoy their meal while overlooking the yachts and shimmering waters.
2. **Ney Restaurant**
   Situated in İçmeler, Ney offers a relaxed atmosphere with a focus on freshly grilled fish and local seafood specialties. Their calamari is a must-try.
3. **Pineapple Restaurant**
   A long-standing favorite, Pineapple combines excellent service with a varied menu, featuring everything from classic grilled fish to seafood pasta.

Why Dine by the Coast?

- **Scenic Ambiance**: Enjoy the gentle sound of waves and cool sea breezes as you dine.
- **Ultra-Fresh Ingredients**: Many restaurants source their seafood from local fishermen, ensuring unparalleled freshness.
- **Perfect for Special Occasions**: Coastal dining is an ideal choice for romantic dinners or celebrations.

Conclusion: Marmaris' seafood restaurants elevate dining into a sensory experience, blending the best of nature and culinary artistry.

9.3 Cafes, Bars, and Street Food

A Flavorful Exploration

For a more casual and diverse dining experience, Marmaris' cafes, bars, and street food stalls are the way to go. These establishments offer everything from quick bites to leisurely meals, catering to every craving.

Cafes

Marmaris boasts a vibrant cafe culture, where you can unwind with a cup of Turkish tea or coffee.

- **Recommended Cafes**:
    - **Kahve Dünyası**: Known for its rich Turkish coffee and delightful pastries.
    - **Cafe Greco**: A modern spot with international coffee blends and great views of the marina.
    - **Sultan's Coffee House**: Perfect for a traditional coffee experience.

Bars

As the sun sets, Marmaris transforms into a lively hub for nightlife. Beachside bars and rooftop lounges serve creative cocktails and ice-cold beers, often accompanied by live music.

- **Recommended Bars**:
    - **Bar Street**: Famous for its array of clubs and bars, this area is perfect for party-goers.
    - **Anchor Bar**: A relaxed spot with stunning views and delicious cocktails.

- ○ **Rock Bar Marmaris**: Known for its laid-back vibe and rock music playlist.

Street Food

For foodies on the go, Marmaris' street food scene offers quick, affordable, and mouthwatering options.

1. **Simit**
   This sesame-covered bread ring is a Turkish classic, often enjoyed as a snack or light breakfast.
2. **Kokoreç**
   Grilled seasoned lamb intestines served on bread, this dish is a favorite among locals.
3. **Döner Kebab**
   Juicy slices of meat wrapped in flatbread with vegetables and sauces—a global Turkish favorite.
4. **Corn on the Cob**
   Roasted or boiled corn is a common street snack, sold from brightly colored carts.
5. **Ice Cream (Dondurma)**
   Turkish ice cream vendors are known for their entertaining antics and creamy, stretchy treats.

Why Explore Cafes, Bars, and Street Food?

- **Affordability**: Street food and cafes offer budget-friendly options without compromising on taste.
- **Cultural Insight**: Eating where the locals eat gives you a glimpse into daily life in Marmaris.

- **Diverse Offerings**: From sweet to savory, there's always something to satisfy your cravings.

Conclusion: Marmaris' cafes, bars, and street food stalls bring a lively and flavorful dimension to the dining experience. Whether you're sipping coffee, enjoying cocktails, or indulging in street snacks, these spots add a dynamic flair to your culinary journey.

Dining in Marmaris is an adventure that goes beyond just eating—it's about experiencing the culture, history, and warmth of the people through their food. From authentic Turkish meals to fresh seafood by the coast and vibrant street food scenes, every meal becomes a memorable part of your visit.

CHAPTER 10: Nightlife and Entertainment

Marmaris, by day, is a serene paradise of beaches and natural beauty, but when the sun sets, the town transforms into a hub of vibrant nightlife and entertainment. Whether you're in the mood for pulsating dance floors, live music, or a tranquil evening cruise under the stars, Marmaris offers unforgettable nighttime experiences. This chapter delves into the dynamic options for evening entertainment that cater to every taste.

10.1 Nightclubs and Bars

The Heartbeat of Marmaris After Dark

Marmaris is famous for its energetic nightlife scene, centered around its iconic Bar Street and waterfront venues. The town's clubs and bars are diverse, ranging from laid-back lounges to electrifying dance spots, ensuring something for everyone.

Bar Street – The Epicenter of Nightlife

Located near the marina, Bar Street is a vibrant strip packed with an array of nightclubs and bars. It's the go-to destination for partygoers looking to dance the night away. The atmosphere is electric, with neon lights, loud music, and an energetic crowd that keeps the party going until the early hours of the morning.

- **Popular Clubs and Bars on Bar Street**:
  - **Club Areena**: The largest open-air nightclub in Marmaris, offering world-class DJ performances, laser shows, and a massive dance floor.
  - **Crazy Daisy**: Known for its high-energy vibe and international music.
  - **Backstreet Club**: A smaller venue offering a more intimate party atmosphere with great beats.
  - **Joy Club**: Perfect for those who love a mix of dance, R&B, and house music.

Beachfront Bars

If you prefer a more relaxed evening with the sound of waves as your backdrop, the beachfront bars along Marmaris' coast offer a chill alternative.

- **Top Picks**:
  - **Istanbul Beach Bar**: A cozy spot where you can sip cocktails while lounging by the water.
  - **The Red Piano**: Famous for its colorful cocktails and live performances in a friendly, casual setting.

Why Experience Marmaris' Nightclubs and Bars?

- **Variety**: From wild parties to quiet drinks, there's a venue for every mood.

- **Ambiance**: Marmaris' nightlife blends the excitement of modern clubs with the charm of seaside venues.
- **Global Appeal**: Many establishments cater to an international crowd, offering a mix of Turkish and global music.

Pro Tip: Start your evening with a sunset cocktail at a beach bar before heading to Bar Street for the full Marmaris nightlife experience.

10.2 Live Music and Performances

Feel the Rhythm of Marmaris

Marmaris is not just about dancing; it's also a fantastic destination for live music lovers. From traditional Turkish tunes to international hits, the town's live music venues and performance spaces add a cultural and artistic flair to its nightlife.

Turkish Nights and Traditional Performances

For an authentic cultural experience, many restaurants and venues host Turkish nights, featuring live folk music, traditional dances, and belly dancing performances.

- **Recommended Venues**:
    - **Kervansaray Turkish Night Show**: A popular dinner theater where you can enjoy a feast of Turkish cuisine while

watching vibrant folkloric dances and belly dancing.
- **Armutalan Cultural Center**: Hosts occasional cultural shows, including Sufi music and whirling dervish performances.

Live Music Bars

Several bars in Marmaris feature live bands and solo performers, catering to a variety of musical tastes.

- **Notable Spots**:
  - **Bono Good Times Beach**: A trendy beachfront venue offering live jazz, blues, and acoustic sessions in a laid-back atmosphere.
  - **Murphy's Bar**: Known for its lively atmosphere and bands playing classic rock and pop hits.
  - **The Old Town Tavern**: A cozy pub with frequent live performances by local artists.

Theater and Open-Air Shows

During the summer months, Marmaris occasionally hosts open-air theater performances and concerts in its parks and amphitheaters. These events often feature Turkish and international artists, providing a unique entertainment option under the stars.

Why Choose Live Music and Performances?

- **Authenticity**: Turkish nights offer a genuine glimpse into the country's cultural heritage.
- **Relaxation**: Enjoying live music is a more laid-back way to experience Marmaris' nightlife.
- **Variety**: From intimate gigs to large-scale performances, there's something for everyone.

Pro Tip: Check local event listings to catch special performances or seasonal shows during your visit.

10.3 Evening Cruises and Fireworks

An Enchanting End to Your Day

For those who prefer a quieter and more romantic evening, Marmaris offers a variety of evening cruises that allow you to experience the town's beauty from the water. These cruises often include dinner, drinks, and entertainment, creating a magical atmosphere.

Evening Cruises

1. **Dinner Cruises**
   Most evening cruises feature a delicious buffet or multi-course dinner, often showcasing fresh seafood and local specialties. The combination of great food and stunning sea views is unbeatable.
   - **Highlights**: Sunset views, starlit skies, and relaxing sea breezes.
   - **Recommended Operators**:
     - **Blue Voyage Cruises**: Known for their elegant boats and gourmet menus.

- **Marmaris Yacht Tours**: Offers private and group options tailored to different budgets.
    - **Tip**: Book in advance during the high season to secure your spot.
2. **Party Cruises**
   If you'd rather keep the party vibe going on the water, Marmaris also offers lively party cruises featuring DJs, dancing, and themed nights.
    - **Highlights**: Glow parties, foam parties, and great music.
    - **Popular Choice**: **Bar Street Party Boat**, which brings the energy of the club scene to the sea.

Fireworks Displays

Marmaris occasionally hosts fireworks displays, especially during festivals and holidays. Watching fireworks light up the night sky over the marina or from the deck of a boat is an unforgettable experience.

- **Best Viewing Spots**:
    - Marmaris Marina.
    - İçmeler Beach.
    - Onboard an evening cruise.

Why Opt for Evening Cruises?

- **Romance**: Perfect for couples looking for a unique and intimate experience.
- **Scenic Beauty**: Marmaris' coastline is even more stunning when illuminated at night.

- **Memorable Atmosphere**: The combination of sea, stars, and entertainment creates lasting memories.

Pro Tip: Choose a cruise that aligns with your preferences, whether it's a quiet dinner or a high-energy party.

Conclusion

Marmaris' nightlife and entertainment options cater to a wide spectrum of interests, making it a destination that truly comes alive after dark. Whether you're dancing the night away in a pulsating nightclub, enjoying the soulful melodies of live music, or soaking in the serenity of an evening cruise, Marmaris offers unforgettable experiences for every type of traveler. As you explore the town's vibrant after-dark offerings, you'll discover that Marmaris doesn't just sleep under the stars—it thrives.

CHAPTER 11: Shopping in Marmaris

Shopping in Marmaris is a delightful adventure, offering a blend of traditional Turkish culture and modern retail experiences. Whether you're hunting for authentic handicrafts, unique souvenirs, or stylish apparel, this bustling town has something to cater to every shopper's tastes and budget. From vibrant bazaars to chic boutiques, Marmaris presents a shopping journey that's as exciting as its beaches and nightlife.

11.1 Local Markets and Handicrafts

The Heartbeat of Turkish Culture

Exploring Marmaris' local markets is an immersive experience that allows visitors to connect with the town's culture, traditions, and artisans. The

marketplaces here are vibrant and colorful, buzzing with energy as locals and tourists haggle over an array of goods. These markets are not just places to shop but cultural hubs where you can discover Turkey's rich heritage through its crafts and produce.

Grand Bazaar (Marmaris Çarşısı)

One of the most famous markets in Marmaris, the Grand Bazaar is a labyrinth of stalls selling everything from textiles to jewelry. Located near the marina, this bustling market is a must-visit for its sheer variety and lively atmosphere.

- **What to Find**:
    - Handwoven rugs and kilims.
    - Leather goods such as bags, belts, and jackets.
    - Traditional Turkish ceramics with intricate hand-painted designs.
    - Copperware, including teapots and trays.
- **Tips for Shopping**:
    - Bargaining is expected and can be part of the fun! Start with a lower offer and negotiate your way up.
    - Keep an eye out for stalls offering handmade items, as these often provide better quality and a unique touch.

Armutalan Market

Held weekly, this market is smaller and less crowded than the Grand Bazaar, making it an excellent option for those seeking a more relaxed shopping experience. Armutalan Market is particularly famous for its fresh produce and local delicacies.

- **What to Find**:
    - Organic fruits, vegetables, and spices.
    - Honey from local beekeepers.
    - Homemade jams and olive oil.

Içmeler Market

Located a short drive from Marmaris, Içmeler Market operates on Wednesdays and offers a mix of textiles, souvenirs, and household goods.

- **What to Find**:
    - Colorful scarves and shawls.
    - Hand-embroidered tablecloths and linens.
    - Trinkets and keepsakes perfect for gifts.

Handicrafts and Artisans

Marmaris is home to skilled artisans who specialize in traditional crafts. Local workshops and pop-up stalls often feature handmade jewelry, pottery, and even custom-made sandals. Supporting these artisans is a great way to take home a meaningful souvenir while contributing to the local economy.

Why Visit Local Markets?

- **Cultural Immersion**: Markets are a window into Turkish life and traditions.
- **Unique Finds**: Discover one-of-a-kind items you won't find in modern stores.
- **Affordable Prices**: With good bargaining skills, you can get high-quality goods at reasonable rates.

11.2 Modern Malls and Boutiques

A Blend of Style and Comfort

For those who prefer air-conditioned comfort and fixed prices, Marmaris has several modern malls and boutique stores that offer a more contemporary shopping experience. These venues cater to those looking for high-end fashion, branded goods, or stylish home decor.

Blue Port Shopping Mall

Blue Port is one of the largest shopping malls in Marmaris, located conveniently along the main road. With a mix of Turkish and international brands, this mall is a favorite among both locals and tourists.

- **What to Find**:
    - Fashion outlets for clothing, shoes, and accessories.
    - Electronics and gadgets.
    - Cafes and eateries for a shopping break.

Point Center

Smaller than Blue Port but equally appealing, Point Center offers a selection of boutiques and stores selling quality items. It's a great spot for picking up casual wear or unique gifts.

- **Highlights**:
    - Quirky gift shops.
    - Turkish chain stores offering affordable fashion.

Boutique Shopping

Marmaris has a thriving boutique scene, with many shops specializing in niche items such as handmade leather shoes, jewelry, and home decor.

- **Recommended Boutiques**:
    - **Alara Jewelry**: Known for its exquisite gold and silver pieces.
    - **Zen Leather**: Offers custom-made leather jackets and bags.
    - **Ephesus Art House**: A haven for art lovers, featuring prints, sculptures, and artisan crafts.

Why Choose Modern Malls and Boutiques?

- **Convenience**: All your shopping needs under one roof.
- **Quality Assurance**: Products come with clear pricing and guarantees.
- **Trendy Options**: Stay updated with the latest styles and trends.

11.3 What to Buy: Souvenirs and Specialties

Bring Home a Piece of Marmaris

Shopping in Marmaris wouldn't be complete without picking up some unique souvenirs and specialty items to remind you of your visit. From aromatic spices to handcrafted keepsakes, here's what to look out for:

1. Turkish Carpets and Rugs

Turkish rugs are renowned worldwide for their intricate designs and craftsmanship. Whether you're looking for a large carpet or a smaller kilim, Marmaris' markets and stores offer a variety of options.

- **Tip**: Ask about the origin and material of the rug to ensure authenticity.

2. Turkish Delight (Lokum)

No trip to Turkey is complete without sampling Turkish delight. Marmaris offers a variety of flavors, including rose, pistachio, and pomegranate.

- **Where to Buy**: Specialty sweet shops or bazaars.

3. Spices and Herbs

Turkish cuisine is rich in flavors, and you can take some of that magic home by purchasing spices like saffron, sumac, and paprika.

- **Packaging**: Look for vacuum-sealed options to preserve freshness.

4. Olive Oil and Soap

Marmaris is located in a region famous for its olive groves. High-quality olive oil and artisanal olive soap make for thoughtful and practical gifts.

5. Jewelry

From silver bracelets to turquoise necklaces, Marmaris is an excellent place to find unique jewelry pieces that reflect Turkish craftsmanship.

6. Textiles

Pick up handwoven shawls, embroidered pillowcases, or colorful beach towels as a stylish memento of your trip.

7. Ceramics

Hand-painted bowls, plates, and vases in traditional Turkish designs are both beautiful and functional.

How to Ensure Quality

- **Look for Handmade Labels**: Items marked as handmade or locally produced are often higher quality.
- **Ask for Certificates**: For high-value items like rugs and jewelry, request an authenticity certificate.

Conclusion

Shopping in Marmaris is more than a transactional experience—it's a journey through the town's vibrant culture, artistry, and modern charm. Whether you're haggling in the lively markets, browsing the shelves of a boutique, or indulging in retail therapy at a mall, Marmaris offers endless opportunities to find treasures that will remind you of your time in this coastal paradise.

Chapter 12: Seasonal Highlights and Events

12.1 Best Time to Visit Marmaris

Marmaris, a stunning coastal destination in Turkey, offers visitors an ever-changing tapestry of experiences throughout the year. Its Mediterranean climate ensures warm summers and mild winters, making it a year-round attraction. However, the best time to visit depends on your preferences for weather, activities, and crowd sizes.

Spring Awakens Marmaris: March to May
 Spring in Marmaris is a magical time when the town emerges from its winter slumber. The temperatures are comfortably mild, averaging between 15°C and 25°C (59°F to 77°F), making it ideal for outdoor activities. The landscape comes alive with blooming wildflowers, creating a vibrant backdrop for hiking or cycling. Visitors who prefer peaceful, less crowded experiences will find spring particularly appealing. Beaches are serene, and local markets are buzzing with fresh produce and crafts.

Spring is also when Marmaris begins to host events, such as the Marmaris International Yacht Charter Show in May. This prestigious gathering of yachts and maritime enthusiasts sets the tone for the sailing season, offering an excellent opportunity to explore Marmaris' renowned marina and coastline.

Summer Vibes: June to August

Summer is peak season in Marmaris, with temperatures soaring to 30°C to 40°C (86°F to 104°F). The sun-drenched beaches are perfect for sunbathing, swimming, and watersports. The nightlife thrives during this period, with beach clubs, bars, and restaurants offering vibrant entertainment that stretches into the early hours.

However, the bustling crowds might be overwhelming for some travelers. If you plan to visit during the summer, early bookings for accommodations and excursions are essential. Despite the higher prices and busy streets, the energy of Marmaris in summer is unmatched, making it an excellent choice for party lovers and families seeking fun-filled vacations.

Autumn Serenity: September to November

As summer crowds dwindle, Marmaris enters a more tranquil phase. The autumn months are an excellent time for those seeking a relaxed vacation. Temperatures range from 20°C to 30°C (68°F to 86°F), offering perfect conditions for outdoor activities like hiking in the Marmaris National Park or exploring ancient ruins nearby.

The sea remains warm enough for swimming well into October, while local vineyards offer wine-tasting experiences during the harvest season. Autumn is also a time to savor Marmaris' culinary delights, as seafood and local produce are at their freshest.

Winter Charm: December to February
While Marmaris is quieter in winter, it still holds charm for travelers looking for a peaceful retreat. Daytime temperatures hover around 15°C to 20°C (59°F to 68°F), suitable for sightseeing and exploring the town's cultural landmarks. Winter is a time for discounted accommodations and fewer crowds, making it a budget-friendly option.

Though some attractions and restaurants may close during the off-season, Marmaris' natural beauty remains undiminished. The serene ambiance and scenic trails provide a unique perspective of this vibrant destination, away from the summer frenzy.

12.2 Festivals and Celebrations

Marmaris is not just about pristine beaches and scenic beauty; its rich cultural tapestry is brought to life through its festivals and celebrations. These events reflect the local heritage, communal spirit, and vibrant traditions, offering visitors an immersive experience.

Marmaris Maritime and Spring Festival
Held annually in May, the Marmaris Maritime and Spring Festival marks the beginning of the tourist season. This lively event features boat parades, live music, folk dance performances, and street food stalls. The festival's highlight is its regatta, where sailing enthusiasts compete along the turquoise coast, providing a spectacular sight for onlookers.

International Marmaris Yacht Races
In October, Marmaris hosts the International Yacht Races, attracting sailors and spectators from around the

globe. This prestigious event showcases the maritime prowess of the region and fosters camaraderie among participants. Visitors can enjoy the vibrant atmosphere of the marina, which comes alive with concerts, exhibitions, and festive dinners during the event.

Turkish Republic Day Celebrations
October 29th marks Turkish Republic Day, a national holiday celebrated with great enthusiasm in Marmaris. The day is filled with parades, concerts, and fireworks, creating a patriotic ambiance. For visitors, it's an opportunity to witness Turkish pride and partake in the festivities alongside locals.

Local Cultural Festivals
Marmaris also hosts smaller, community-driven festivals throughout the year. These include traditional dance and music showcases, agricultural fairs, and food festivals celebrating regional flavors. One such event is the Olive Harvest Festival in nearby villages, where visitors can learn about olive oil production and enjoy tastings.

New Year's Eve by the Sea
For those celebrating New Year's Eve in Marmaris, the marina is the place to be. With its festive lights, lively music, and waterfront fireworks display, it's a memorable way to ring in the new year.

12.3 Seasonal Activities

The changing seasons bring diverse activities to Marmaris, ensuring there's always something exciting to do, no matter when you visit.

Spring Adventures
Spring is the ideal season for outdoor enthusiasts. The cooler temperatures and blooming flora set the stage for hiking in the Marmaris National Park or biking along scenic trails. Visitors can also take guided tours to ancient sites like Amos and Knidos, where history and nature converge.

Spring is also perfect for birdwatching, as migratory birds pass through Marmaris' wetlands. For water lovers, kayaking and paddleboarding are serene ways to explore the coastline before the summer crowds arrive.

Summer Thrills
Summer is synonymous with beach fun and watersports. Visitors can indulge in activities such as jet skiing, parasailing, and scuba diving. The vibrant underwater world of Marmaris, teeming with marine life and shipwrecks, is a diver's paradise.

Boat trips to nearby islands and bays, like Cleopatra Island or the Blue Lagoon, are a must-do. These excursions often include stops for snorkeling and swimming in crystal-clear waters.

Autumn Exploration
The milder temperatures of autumn make it the best season for exploring Marmaris on foot or by bike. The Lycian Way, a renowned long-distance trail, offers breathtaking views of the coast and opportunities to visit lesser-known villages.

Wine enthusiasts can take part in grape harvest tours at local vineyards, while food lovers can attend seasonal cooking workshops to learn about traditional Turkish cuisine. Sailing also continues to be a popular activity in autumn, with calmer seas and fewer boats.

Winter Retreat

Winter offers a quieter, reflective side of Marmaris. It's an excellent time to enjoy spa treatments and traditional Turkish baths. Cultural enthusiasts can visit the Marmaris Castle and Museum or take day trips to Ephesus and Pamukkale.

Fishing enthusiasts will find winter rewarding, as it's the season for catching fresh fish in Marmaris' waters. Meanwhile, local markets and workshops provide an opportunity to connect with artisans and purchase handmade goods.

Each season in Marmaris offers unique charms and activities, ensuring an unforgettable experience tailored to every traveler's preferences. From festive celebrations to serene winter retreats, Marmaris invites you to explore its treasures year-round.

Chapter 13: Practical Information for Travelers

13.1 Currency and Payment Methods

Marmaris, like the rest of Turkey, uses the Turkish Lira (TRY) as its official currency. Understanding currency and payment options is crucial for a hassle-free trip, ensuring you can navigate daily expenses smoothly.

Currency Overview
The Turkish Lira is available in denominations of banknotes (5, 10, 20, 50, 100, and 200 lira) and coins (1 lira and smaller kuruş coins). Familiarize yourself with these to avoid confusion during transactions. Currency exchange rates fluctuate, so it's wise to check the current rate before converting money.

Exchanging Currency

You can exchange foreign currency at banks, exchange offices (döviz), and some hotels. Exchange offices in Marmaris offer competitive rates, especially in tourist areas like the marina and central markets. Banks typically operate Monday to Friday from 9:00 AM to 5:00 PM, but exchange offices often have extended hours.

It's advisable to avoid exchanging money at airports, as they often have less favorable rates. Carry small denominations of lira for convenience, particularly when shopping at local markets or using public transportation.

Payment Methods

Credit and debit cards are widely accepted in Marmaris, especially in hotels, restaurants, and larger stores. Visa and Mastercard are the most commonly accepted cards, while American Express may not be as widely used. Ensure your card has international transaction capabilities, and inform your bank of your travel plans to avoid disruptions.

For smaller establishments, street vendors, and local markets, cash is the preferred payment method. ATMs are abundant in Marmaris, dispensing Turkish Lira. Many ATMs offer language options, including English, making them user-friendly for tourists.

Tipping and Service Charges

Tipping, known as "bahşiş," is customary in Turkey. In restaurants, a 10% to 15% tip is appreciated if a service charge is not already included. For taxi drivers, rounding up the fare is common. Hotel staff, such as porters and housekeeping, often receive small tips as a token of gratitude.

Mobile Payment Options
Mobile payment apps and digital wallets are gaining popularity in Turkey, though they are more common in larger cities. If you plan to use mobile payment methods, check if they are compatible with Turkish systems.

13.2 Local Customs and Etiquette

Understanding local customs and etiquette in Marmaris is essential to show respect for Turkish culture and create positive interactions with locals.

Greetings and Social Norms
Greetings are a vital part of Turkish culture. A handshake is the most common form of greeting among strangers, while close friends may exchange kisses on both cheeks. Addressing people respectfully, using titles like "Bey" (Mr.) and "Hanım" (Mrs./Ms.) after their first names, is considered polite.

Hospitality and Invitations
Turkish people are renowned for their hospitality. If invited to someone's home, it's customary to bring a small gift, such as sweets or flowers. Removing your shoes before entering a home is standard practice.

Dress Code
While Marmaris is a tourist-friendly destination with relaxed dress codes, modest attire is recommended when

visiting religious sites, such as mosques. Women should cover their heads, shoulders, and knees, while men should avoid wearing shorts inside these sacred places.

Public Behavior
Public displays of affection should be kept to a minimum, as they may be frowned upon in more conservative areas. Smoking is common in Turkey but is prohibited in indoor public spaces. Always ask for permission before taking photographs of people, particularly in rural areas.

Market Etiquette
Haggling is a common practice in markets and bazaars. Approach it with a friendly demeanor and a willingness to negotiate. Vendors expect bargaining, and it can be a fun way to interact with locals.

Religious Sensitivities
Turkey is a predominantly Muslim country. During Ramadan, the holy month of fasting, it's respectful to avoid eating, drinking, or smoking in public during daylight hours. However, tourist areas like Marmaris are more lenient.

13.3 Emergency Numbers and Safety Tips

Staying informed about emergency contacts and safety measures ensures peace of mind while exploring Marmaris.

Emergency Numbers

- **Police**: 155
- **Ambulance**: 112
- **Fire Brigade**: 110
- **Coast Guard**: 158

These numbers are toll-free and accessible nationwide. For non-Turkish speakers, some operators may provide assistance in English.

Health and Medical Services

Marmaris has several hospitals and clinics, including private facilities that cater to tourists. Pharmacies, known as "eczane," are plentiful and can provide over-the-counter medications. Most pharmacies have a rotating schedule for after-hours services.

Travel insurance is essential to cover unforeseen medical expenses. Ensure your policy includes coverage for adventure activities like diving or hiking if you plan to engage in them.

Safety Tips

Marmaris is generally a safe destination, but staying vigilant is always advisable. Here are some tips:

- Avoid carrying large sums of cash and keep valuables secure.
- Use official taxis or reputable ride-sharing apps.
- Stay hydrated and use sunscreen, especially during summer.
- Be cautious of pickpockets in crowded areas like markets and beaches.

Natural Hazards
Marmaris is located in an earthquake-prone region. Familiarize yourself with safety protocols, and stay updated on local alerts. During water activities, follow safety guidelines and heed instructions from tour operators.

13.4 Language Tips and Useful Phrases

While English is widely spoken in Marmaris, especially in tourist areas, learning a few Turkish phrases can enrich your experience and foster goodwill with locals.

Common Turkish Phrases

- **Hello**: Merhaba
- **Good morning**: Günaydın
- **Thank you**: Teşekkür ederim
- **Yes/No**: Evet/Hayır
- **Please**: Lütfen
- **Excuse me/Sorry**: Affedersiniz
- **How much?**: Ne kadar?
- **I don't understand**: Anlamıyorum
- **Do you speak English?**: İngilizce konuşuyor musunuz?
- **Goodbye**: Hoşça kalın

Pronunciation Tips
Turkish is a phonetic language, meaning words are pronounced as they are written. Learning the Turkish alphabet can help with accurate pronunciation. For

example, the letter "ç" is pronounced like "ch" in "church," and "ş" sounds like "sh" in "shoe."

Language Etiquette
Making an effort to speak Turkish, even if only a few words, is appreciated by locals. It shows respect for their culture and often results in warmer interactions.

Translation Apps and Guides
While translation apps can be helpful, carrying a pocket-sized Turkish phrasebook is a good backup. Offline apps are particularly useful in areas with limited connectivity.

Each of these practical insights ensures that travelers to Marmaris are well-prepared to navigate the destination with confidence and ease, enhancing their overall experience.

Chapter 14: Sustainability and Responsible Tourism

Tourism in Marmaris offers an opportunity to enjoy breathtaking landscapes, cultural heritage, and a vibrant local community. However, as a responsible traveler, you can also play a vital role in ensuring that this beauty is preserved for generations to come. Practicing sustainability and embracing responsible tourism allows you to minimize your impact while positively contributing to the region.

14.1 Supporting Local Businesses

Marmaris thrives on a blend of tourism and local enterprise. By supporting small businesses, you not only experience authentic Turkish culture but also help sustain the community's economic vitality.

Shop Locally
Marmaris is renowned for its charming bazaars and artisan markets. The Marmaris Grand Bazaar, for example, is an excellent place to purchase handmade

goods such as carpets, leather products, and jewelry. Opt for locally crafted items over mass-produced souvenirs to directly support local artisans. These products often reflect the cultural heritage of the region, adding a meaningful touch to your purchase.

Eat at Local Restaurants
Dining at family-run establishments and traditional Turkish eateries helps the local economy. Instead of frequenting international chains, choose local restaurants that serve dishes like *mezes*, *kebabs*, and freshly caught seafood. Marmaris's markets also offer a rich array of fresh produce, allowing you to savor the flavors of the region while supporting local farmers.

Stay in Locally Owned Accommodations
While luxury resorts are common in Marmaris, consider staying in locally owned boutique hotels, guesthouses, or eco-lodges. These accommodations often have a smaller ecological footprint and foster a more personal connection with the region. Many also use locally sourced materials and employ residents, further benefiting the community.

Participate in Community-Based Tourism
Engage with local culture through community-driven initiatives. Workshops on Turkish cooking, pottery, or traditional dance offer immersive experiences while providing locals with income opportunities. Guided tours led by residents provide a unique perspective on Marmaris's history and natural beauty.

14.2 Eco-Friendly Activities

Marmaris offers plenty of activities for eco-conscious travelers, blending adventure with a respect for the environment.

Hiking and Nature Walks
Explore the lush trails of the Marmaris National Park or the scenic paths leading to nearby villages like Turunç. Hiking allows you to enjoy Marmaris's diverse landscapes without leaving a carbon footprint. Respect trail guidelines by staying on marked paths and avoiding disturbances to local wildlife.

Water-Based Adventures
Marmaris's coastline is perfect for eco-friendly water activities such as kayaking, paddleboarding, and sailing. These low-impact options offer a sustainable alternative to motorized water sports, which can harm marine ecosystems. When snorkeling or diving, be cautious around coral reefs and avoid touching marine life.

Bicycle Rentals
Cycling is a fantastic way to explore Marmaris. The town has several bike rental shops and dedicated cycling paths, allowing you to enjoy the sights while reducing emissions. Popular cycling routes include the seaside promenade and trails through the countryside.

Visit Conservation Areas
Marmaris is home to several protected areas, such as the Dalyan Delta and Iztuzu Beach, famous for its nesting loggerhead turtles (Caretta caretta). By visiting these sites, you contribute to conservation efforts and learn about the importance of preserving these habitats. Choose eco-certified tours that prioritize animal welfare and environmental sustainability.

Support Renewable Energy Initiatives
Some tour operators and accommodations in Marmaris have adopted renewable energy practices. Opt for businesses that use solar panels, water conservation systems, and energy-efficient operations.

14.3 Protecting Marmaris' Natural Beauty

Marmaris's charm lies in its pristine beaches, turquoise waters, and lush landscapes. Protecting these natural treasures is a shared responsibility that every visitor can embrace.

Reduce Plastic Use
Plastic waste is a significant environmental challenge in tourist-heavy destinations. Carry a reusable water bottle and refill it at designated stations or with filtered water available in hotels. Bring a reusable shopping bag for purchases and avoid single-use plastics whenever possible.

Dispose of Waste Responsibly
Ensure that your trash is disposed of in designated bins. Many beaches and parks in Marmaris have recycling facilities—use them appropriately. Participate in local beach clean-up initiatives, which are often organized by community groups or environmental organizations.

Respect Wildlife and Flora
Avoid disturbing wildlife by maintaining a safe distance and not feeding animals. Protect the local flora by refraining from picking plants or flowers, which may be crucial to the ecosystem. In marine environments, be

cautious about coral reefs, as they are delicate and slow-growing.

Conserve Water and Energy
Water scarcity can be a concern in tourist destinations. Take short showers, turn off taps while brushing your teeth, and reuse towels in hotels to minimize water waste. Similarly, conserve energy by switching off lights and air conditioning when not in use.

Support Eco-Tourism Operators
When booking tours, prioritize companies that follow sustainable practices, such as limiting group sizes, avoiding environmentally sensitive areas, and educating participants about conservation. Look for certifications like Travelife or Green Key, which indicate a commitment to sustainability.

Raise Awareness
Share your experiences and knowledge about sustainable tourism with fellow travelers and on social media platforms. Highlight responsible practices and encourage others to adopt them during their visit to Marmaris.

Embracing sustainability in Marmaris doesn't mean compromising on the enjoyment of your trip. By supporting local businesses, engaging in eco-friendly activities, and taking steps to protect the environment, you contribute to preserving this paradise for future travelers. Through conscious choices, you become part of the global movement toward responsible tourism, ensuring that Marmaris's natural beauty and cultural heritage remain vibrant and accessible for generations to come.

Chapter 15: Planning Your Marmaris Itinerary

Whether you're visiting Marmaris for a few days, a week, or planning an extended stay, careful planning ensures that you make the most of this stunning coastal destination. Marmaris offers something for every traveler—from scenic beaches and vibrant nightlife to tranquil hikes and cultural explorations. In this chapter, we provide detailed itineraries and tips to help you organize your trip, whether it's a short visit or a long-term adventure.

15.1 Suggested 3-Day Itinerary

A three-day trip to Marmaris is perfect for those seeking a quick escape. This itinerary balances relaxation, exploration, and cultural immersion.

Day 1: Arrival and Marmaris Marina

- **Morning:** Arrive in Marmaris and check into your accommodation. Choose a hotel near the Marina for easy access to the town's main attractions. Start your day with a leisurely breakfast at a café overlooking the sea.
- **Afternoon:** Begin your exploration at Marmaris Castle and Museum. The castle offers panoramic views of the coastline and houses fascinating exhibits on the town's history. Stroll along the Marmaris Marina, where luxury yachts and traditional Turkish *gulets* create a picturesque backdrop.
- **Evening:** Enjoy dinner at a seafood restaurant by the waterfront. Try local dishes like grilled sea bream or calamari. Wrap up your day with a sunset cruise along the coastline, a perfect introduction to Marmaris's beauty.

Day 2: Beaches and Nature

- **Morning:** Head to Icmeler Beach, just a short drive from Marmaris. This family-friendly beach

offers golden sands, crystal-clear waters, and plenty of water sports options like kayaking and paddleboarding.
- **Afternoon:** Explore Marmaris National Park. Hike through the lush trails, keeping an eye out for native flora and fauna. Pack a picnic to enjoy amidst the serene natural surroundings.
- **Evening:** Return to Marmaris town and visit the Grand Bazaar for some shopping. Pick up unique souvenirs like Turkish ceramics or spices. Finish your day at a traditional Turkish restaurant, enjoying dishes like *adana kebab* and *meze*.

Day 3: Boat Trips and Dalyan Excursion

- **Morning:** Spend your final day on a boat trip. Many tours offer stops at secluded coves, snorkel-friendly waters, and Turtle Beach. Alternatively, opt for a day trip to Dalyan, where you can visit the famous mud baths and the ancient Lycian rock tombs.
- **Afternoon:** In Dalyan, enjoy a relaxing boat ride along the Dalyan River. Have lunch at a riverside café, savoring fresh seafood and Turkish tea.
- **Evening:** Return to Marmaris and unwind with a walk along the promenade. Cap off your trip with a nightcap at a lively bar or a peaceful moment by the sea.

15.2 One-Week Stay: A Balanced Adventure

A week in Marmaris allows you to dive deeper into its attractions while balancing adventure with relaxation.

Day 1–3: Follow the 3-Day Itinerary

Day 4: Explore Turunç and Local Villages

- **Morning:** Visit the charming village of Turunç, accessible by a short ferry ride or a scenic drive. Its quiet beach and small-town vibe offer a contrast to Marmaris's bustling atmosphere.
- **Afternoon:** Tour nearby villages like Bayır, where you can experience authentic Turkish hospitality and sample local honey. Stop by the ancient plane tree in Bayır Square, believed to bring good luck.
- **Evening:** Return to Marmaris for a relaxing dinner. Try *lahmacun*, a thin Turkish pizza, at a casual eatery.

Day 5: Water Adventures

- Spend the day exploring the turquoise waters around Marmaris. Book a snorkeling or diving tour to discover the vibrant marine life. Visit Cleopatra Island, known for its pristine sands and crystal-clear waters. Legend has it that the sand was imported for Cleopatra herself.

Day 6: Cultural Experiences

- **Morning:** Visit local museums and cultural sites. Marmaris's ethnography museum showcases traditional Turkish life, while a visit to the Marmaris Amphitheater offers a glimpse into ancient entertainment.
- **Afternoon:** Take a Turkish cooking class to learn how to prepare local dishes. You'll leave with new skills and a deeper appreciation for Marmaris's culinary heritage.
- **Evening:** Enjoy a traditional Turkish bath (*hamam*) to rejuvenate before your final day.

Day 7: Relaxation and Farewell

- Spend your last day soaking up the sun at Marmaris Beach. For a luxurious treat, book a private cabana or enjoy a beachfront spa session. Take a final walk along the promenade, reflecting on the memories made during your stay.

15.3 Long-Term Travel Tips

For those planning an extended stay in Marmaris, embracing the local lifestyle and exploring beyond the tourist trail can be incredibly rewarding.

Accommodations for Long Stays

- Opt for rental apartments or long-stay guesthouses for a more cost-effective and home-like experience. Look for properties with kitchen

- facilities to prepare your own meals using fresh ingredients from local markets.
- Explore quieter areas like Armutalan or Içmeler for a more peaceful base. These neighborhoods offer a blend of residential charm and easy access to Marmaris's attractions.

Getting Around

- Invest in a *Mugla Kent Kart*, a prepaid transportation card that can be used on local buses. For more flexibility, consider renting a bicycle or scooter.
- Take time to explore lesser-known destinations. The villages surrounding Marmaris, like Bozburun and Selimiye, offer untouched landscapes and authentic cultural experiences.

Building Connections

- Learn a few Turkish phrases to connect with locals. Simple greetings like *Merhaba* (Hello) or *Teşekkür ederim* (Thank you) go a long way.
- Participate in local events and festivals to immerse yourself in Marmaris's culture. Volunteering for community projects or joining workshops can also be fulfilling.

Balancing Work and Leisure

- If you're working remotely, Marmaris offers plenty of coworking spaces and cafes with

reliable Wi-Fi. Choose spots with a view of the marina or the mountains for inspiration.
- Plan your work schedule around off-peak hours to explore Marmaris without crowds. Early mornings and late afternoons are ideal for enjoying the beaches and trails.

Sustainability in Long-Term Travel

- Practice sustainability by supporting local markets, minimizing waste, and conserving energy in your accommodations. Build relationships with local businesses and contribute to the community's well-being.
- Avoid over-tourism by visiting popular sites during weekdays or exploring lesser-visited attractions.

Health and Safety

- Familiarize yourself with local healthcare facilities and emergency numbers. Pharmacies (*eczane*) in Marmaris are well-stocked, and many staff speak English.
- Stay hydrated, especially during the summer months, and wear sunscreen to protect against the strong Mediterranean sun.

Exploring Beyond Marmaris

- Use Marmaris as a base for longer excursions. Day trips to Ephesus, Pamukkale, or Rhodes Island are easily accessible. For longer adventures, consider exploring nearby regions like Fethiye, Bodrum, or Antalya.

Planning your Marmaris itinerary allows you to tailor your experience to your interests and travel style. Whether you're visiting for a weekend, a week, or longer, Marmaris promises a rich blend of natural beauty, cultural heritage, and warm hospitality. With this guide, you'll be well-prepared to create unforgettable memories in this Mediterranean paradise.

Chapter 16: FAQs and Traveler Insights

Marmaris is a popular travel destination celebrated for its turquoise waters, vibrant nightlife, and rich history. In this chapter, we aim to address common questions travelers have, offer insights from seasoned visitors, and provide valuable resources for further exploration. Whether you're planning your first trip to Marmaris or you're a seasoned traveler, this chapter will serve as a comprehensive guide to enhance your journey.

16.1. Common Questions About Marmaris

Travelers often have several queries when considering a visit to Marmaris. Here are answers to some frequently asked questions:

1. What is the best time to visit Marmaris?
Marmaris enjoys a Mediterranean climate, making it an attractive destination year-round. The peak tourist season runs from May to October, offering sunny days and warm waters. For those who prefer fewer crowds and milder weather, visiting in April or November is ideal.

2. How can I get to Marmaris?
Marmaris is well-connected via air, sea, and road. The nearest airport, Dalaman Airport, is approximately 95 kilometers away. From the airport, travelers can take a shuttle, taxi, or car rental to Marmaris. Ferry services

from Rhodes, Greece, also make Marmaris accessible for international travelers.

3. Is Marmaris family-friendly?
Absolutely. Marmaris offers numerous family-friendly activities, including water parks, dolphin shows, and safe beaches. The town's relaxed ambiance and welcoming locals make it an excellent destination for all ages.

4. What are the must-visit attractions in Marmaris?
Some of Marmaris' highlights include Marmaris Castle, the bustling Marina, and Icmeler Beach. Adventurous travelers often explore the nearby Dalyan River or take boat trips to secluded bays and islands.

5. What currency is used in Marmaris, and are cards widely accepted?
The official currency is the Turkish Lira (TRY), but many establishments also accept euros and dollars. Credit and debit cards are widely used, though it's always handy to carry some cash for smaller shops or markets.

6. Is Marmaris safe for solo travelers?
Marmaris is generally safe for all travelers, including those exploring solo. The town has a low crime rate, and locals are known for their hospitality. However, standard safety precautions, like avoiding poorly lit areas at night, are always recommended.

7. What language is spoken, and will I face a language barrier?
Turkish is the primary language spoken in Marmaris,

but English is widely understood, particularly in tourist areas. Learning a few basic Turkish phrases can enhance your experience and endear you to locals.

8. What are the dining options in Marmaris?
Marmaris caters to all culinary preferences, offering traditional Turkish cuisine, seafood, and international dishes. From fine dining restaurants to street food stalls, there's something for every palate and budget.

16.2. Tips from Experienced Visitors

Seasoned travelers to Marmaris share invaluable insights that can make your trip smoother and more enjoyable:

1. Choose the right accommodation.
Marmaris offers a range of lodging options, from luxurious resorts to budget-friendly hostels. Those looking for tranquility may prefer staying in Icmeler, while party enthusiasts often opt for accommodations near Bar Street.

2. Embrace local transportation.
The dolmuş (minibus) is an affordable and convenient way to get around Marmaris and its surrounding areas. Taxis are also available but can be pricier.

3. Explore beyond the main tourist areas.
While Marmaris' town center is vibrant and exciting, nearby villages like Turunc and Selimiye offer a glimpse

into traditional Turkish life. These quieter spots provide a stark contrast to the bustling town and are worth a visit.

4. Pack appropriately for activities.
From hiking trails to water sports, Marmaris offers diverse activities. Pack versatile clothing, comfortable walking shoes, and swimwear to ensure you're prepared for all adventures.

5. Haggle at markets.
Markets in Marmaris are perfect for purchasing souvenirs, textiles, and spices. Bargaining is customary and can lead to great deals. Be polite and persistent but know when to stop.

6. Respect local customs.
While Marmaris is a tourist hub, it's essential to respect Turkish culture. Dress modestly when visiting mosques and be mindful of local traditions during Ramadan.

7. Take a boat trip.
Boat tours are a quintessential Marmaris experience. Opt for smaller, family-operated boats for a more personalized journey. These tours often include stops at hidden bays, snorkeling spots, and meals on board.

8. Stay hydrated and use sun protection.
The Mediterranean sun can be intense, particularly during summer. Always carry water and apply sunscreen to avoid dehydration or sunburn.

9. Use reputable tour operators.
When booking excursions or activities, choose operators

with good reviews to ensure safety and quality. Researching online or asking for recommendations from your accommodation can help.

10. Try local delicacies.
Experienced visitors recommend indulging in Marmaris' culinary delights. Don't miss dishes like gözleme (savory pancakes), fresh seafood, and baklava.

16.3. Resources for Further Reading

Planning a trip to Marmaris becomes easier with access to the right resources. Here are some suggestions for further reading:

1. Travel Guides:

- *Lonely Planet: Turkey* – A comprehensive guide covering Marmaris and beyond.
- *DK Eyewitness Travel Guide: Turkey* – Features detailed maps and stunning photography.

2. Online Forums and Blogs:

- **TripAdvisor**: Offers reviews, recommendations, and forums where travelers share their experiences.
- **Nomadic Matt**: Provides budget travel tips and destination highlights.
- **The Planet D**: Chronicles the adventures of seasoned travelers exploring Marmaris.

3. Local Websites:

- **GoTurkey**: The official tourism website for Turkey, featuring up-to-date information on Marmaris.
- **Marmaris Info**: Offers insights into local events, attractions, and practical tips.

4. Books:

- *Blue Voyage: A Memoir of Sailing Turkey's Turquoise Coast* by Charles Gates – An engaging read for maritime enthusiasts.
- *Turkish Coast: Archaeological and Architectural Highlights* by George Bean – Perfect for history buffs.

5. Social Media Groups:

Platforms like Facebook and Reddit host active communities of travelers sharing Marmaris-specific tips and itineraries. Look for groups like "Turkey Travel Tips" or "Marmaris Vacationers."

6. Language Apps and Tools:

- **Duolingo**: Helps travelers pick up basic Turkish phrases.
- **Google Translate**: Handy for real-time translations.

7. YouTube Channels:

- **Marmaris Life**: Features videos showcasing the town's attractions and local culture.
- **Expats in Turkey**: Provides insights into life as a foreigner in Marmaris.

8. Cultural Resources:

- *Turkey Unveiled* by Nicole and Hugh Pope – A deeper dive into Turkish culture and history.
- *Istanbul to Marmaris: Exploring Turkey's Rich Heritage* by Daniel Jacobs – A detailed exploration of Turkey's southwestern coast.

By addressing common queries, sharing expert tips, and providing further resources, this chapter equips you with the tools to plan an unforgettable Marmaris adventure. Let these insights guide your journey as you discover the magic of this stunning coastal town.

Printed in Dunstable, United Kingdom